ISLAM
AND THE
CROSS

ISLAM AND THE CROSS

SELECTIONS FROM
"THE APOSTLE TO ISLAM"

SAMUEL M. ZWEMER

Edited by ROGER S. GREENWAY

P&R PUBLISHING
P.O.BOX 817 • PHILLIPSBURG • NEW JERSEY 08865-0817

Unless otherwise indicated, all Scripture citations are from the King
James Version (KJV) of the Holy Bible.

Page design by Lakeside Design Plus
Typesetting by Michelle Feaster

Printed in the United States of America

Library of Congress Cataloging-in-Publication Data

Zwemer, Samuel Marinus, 1867–1952.
 Islam and the cross : selections from "the Apostle to Islam" /
Samuel M. Zwemer ; compiled and edited by Roger S. Greenway.
   p. cm.
 Includes bibliographical references and indexes.
 ISBN 0-87552-214-9 (pbk.)
 1. Missions to Muslims—Quotations. 2. Christianity and other
religions—Islam. 3. Islam—Relations—Christianity. 4. Animism.
5. Islam. I. Greenway, Roger S. II. Title.

BV2626.Z8 A25 2002
261.2'7—dc21

                                      2002028538

I wish to express my appreciation to
Albert A. Strydhorst and Anthony J. Meyer
for their assistance in the preparation of this
manuscript during their student days
at Calvin Theological Seminary.

CONTENTS

SOURCES FOR
ISLAM AND THE CROSS

Writings of Samuel M. Zwemer That
Served as Sources of This Book

CHAPTERS   FROM

1–2   *The Moslem Christ.* London: Oliphant. First edi-
              tion, 1912, 8, 114–31 (chapter 1), 155–73
              (chapter 2).

3   *The Cross Above the Crescent.* Grand Rapids,
              Michigan: Zondervan, 1941, 271–81.

4   *Dynamic Christianity and the World Today.* Lon-
              don: The Inter-Varsity Fellowship of Evangel-
              ical Unions, 1939, 81–94.

5   *The Cross Above the Crescent.* Grand Rapids,
              Michigan: Zondervan, 1941, 245–54.

6–9   *The Influence of Animism on Islam.* New York:
              Macmillan, 1920. London: Society for the
              Propagation of Christian Knowledge, 1921,
              1–19 (chapter 6), 107–24 (chapter 7), 87–106
              (chapter 8).

              The Moslem World. Volume 6, 1916, 360–74
              (chapter 7), 236–52 (chapter 8); volume 10,
              1920, 13–24 (chapter 9).

Concl.   *The Call to Prayer.* London: Marshall Brothers,
              1923, 9–52.

INTRODUCTION BY
ROGER S. GREENWAY

N o one through all the centuries of Christian missions to Moslems has deserved better than Samuel Zwemer the designation of *Apostle to Islam*." So wrote the great mission historian, Kenneth Scott Latourette, in the introduction to J. Christy Wilson's biography of Zwemer, published in 1952.

The purpose of this book is to make available to Christians some of Zwemer's insights regarding Islam and its basic differences with Christianity, and to convey his sense of love for Muslim people and passion for their salvation.

In the course of his life, Zwemer published more than fifty books, plus countless articles, editorials, and book reviews. As compiler and editor of this volume, I found it painful to narrow the selection to a mere ten chapters selected from only five of Zwemer's books. Before turning to this sampling of Zwemer material, I want readers to become acquainted with the author and the Muslim world that was the context of his writing.

Samuel Marinus Zwemer was born on April 12, 1867, in the parsonage of the Reformed church in Vriesland, Michigan. His parents had immigrated to America from the Netherlands, and Samuel was the thirteenth of their fifteen children.

The Zwemers were a close-knit family, with deep religious convictions and moral values. All six of Samuel's sisters became schoolteachers, and four of his brothers entered the Christian ministry. One of the brothers died in mission service in Arabia.

Zwemer professed his personal faith in Jesus Christ on March 9, 1884, and he soon became active in the campus mission group at Hope College, the school he attended in Holland, Michigan. In 1887, Robert Wilder visited Hope College as representative of the Student Volunteer Movement, and Zwemer responded to Wilder's appeal for missionaries. It was not until years later that Zwemer learned that when he was still an infant, his mother had dedicated him to missionary service.

After completing his undergraduate work at Hope College, Zwemer went to New Brunswick Seminary in New Jersey for theological studies. Like Hope College, New Brunswick was (and is) owned by the Reformed Church in America. While at seminary, Zwemer joined with two other students, James Cantine and Philip T. Phelps, and a professor of Old Testament who had been a missionary in Egypt, John G. Lansing, to plan a mission to Muslims. The Lord led them to focus on Arabia, the center of the Muslim world and the most difficult place to conduct Christian missions.

In view of the general hostility of Muslims toward Christianity and the difficulties involved in a place like Arabia, it was not surprising that they could not find a mission agency that would sponsor them. So in 1888, while still in school, they decided to form a new agency, which they called the Arabian Mission, under which they could be sent. Zwemer was heard to say, "If God calls you and no board will send you, bore a hole through the board and go anyway." An entrepreneurial spirit, coupled with enormous faith, vision, and energy, characterized Zwemer throughout his life.

In 1890, having finished his seminary education and being ordained, Zwemer sailed to the Middle East, where he joined Cantine in Beirut for the study of the Arabic language. Phelps stayed in the United States as treasurer and fundraiser of the mission. From Beirut, Zwemer and Cantine went to Cairo, Egypt, where they joined Professor Lansing and laid plans for the exploration of Arabia and nearby countries for mission openings. After extensive investigation they settled on Basrah, sixty miles above the Persian Gulf on the combined waterways of the Tigris and Euphrates rivers.

They worked in Basrah for six years, and then a happy event occurred in Zwemer's life. He and Cantine had been asked to meet two young women missionaries who were coming to Basrah from Australia. The Australian mission did not allow single ladies to see male friends, but Zwemer managed to get a job teaching them Arabic. One of the two women was Amy Wilkes, a trained nurse, and she and Zwemer fell in love. In 1896, they were married at the British Consulate in Baghdad. But marriage did not come cheaply for Zwemer, because his bride's mission insisted that he reimburse them for Amy's travel expenses to the field. That led to the report that in good Arab fashion, Zwemer had purchased his wife.

Some time later Zwemer and his wife moved to Bahrain, a British-held island in the Persian Gulf, where they set up a mission station. In Bahrain, Zwemer combined street preaching and literature colportage work on behalf of the American Bible Society with simple medical care. While still in America, Zwemer had done some study of medicine and had worked as a volunteer at a mission clinic in New York City. Now he had Amy, a nurse, to help him, and together they began to practice rudimentary medicine. In 1892, Zwemer's younger brother, Peter, joined them in the mission and opened a substation in Muscat. In 1894 the Arabian Mission was adopted by the board of the Reformed Church and became one of their regular fields.

Zwemer wrote his first book in Bahrain. In the sweltering heat, he wrapped a towel around his hand to keep the perspiration from blotting the ink on the paper. The book, *Arabia: The Cradle of Islam*, went through four editions between 1900 and 1912. The second book written in Bahrain was *Raymond Lull, First Missionary to Moslems*, and this short missionary biography was translated and published in Arabic, Spanish, German, Chinese, and Dutch.

Death touched the Arabian Mission as Peter Zwemer, Samuel's brother, died in 1898. Two daughters born to Samuel and Amy succumbed to dysentery in July 1904. On the tomb that marks their graves on the island of Bahrain appear the words, "Worthy is the Lamb to receive riches."

Zwemer was a powerful speaker as well as a writer. It became known in church and mission circles that Zwemer possessed gifts that enabled him to raise money and recruit new workers. It was not surprising, therefore, that in 1905, while the Zwemers were on furlough in America, Zwemer received two appointments, one to serve as field secretary of the Reformed Board of Foreign Missions, and the second to be the traveling representative for recruitment of the Student Volunteer Movement. He accepted them both. In the latter role, Zwemer worked closely with Robert E. Speer, and the two of them influenced many young men and women to go into overseas missionary service.

In 1910, Zwemer took part in the great World Missionary Conference in Edinburgh, Scotland. During the conference, plans were made to begin a quarterly publication to be called *The Moslem World*. The journal first appeared in January 1911, with Zwemer as the editor. Despite his enormous travel schedule, leadership in numerous conferences, and many other involvements, Zwemer continued as editor without remuneration for thirty-seven years, and he never missed an issue.

With good reason Speer once wrote about Zwemer, "In this century, not many men have lived who had the talent and drive of Samuel Zwemer. He exercised a tremendous influence on the Christian mission to Islam and on the advance of the church and the gospel worldwide."

In the years that followed, Zwemer moved back and forth from Egypt, where he taught at the Presbyterian Seminary, to the Persian Gulf, where he spoke to Muslims and promoted literature distribution and writing. He traveled to the United States, where he spoke hundreds of times to student groups, churches, and missionary conferences. He went country by country across North Africa, then to South Africa at the invitation of the Dutch Reformed Church of South Africa, where he spoke in English and Dutch to Christian congregations and in Arabic to gatherings of Muslims. He went on to Indonesia, where he challenged Christians in Java and Sumatra to increase their mission work among Muslims. Then he was in Baghdad for a conference with missionaries from Arabia, Iran, and Iraq. He went to India, where he spoke at conferences from one side of the country to the other. He made visits to China, where there are millions of Muslims, and in several Chinese cities he was invited to speak in mosques because of his knowledge of Arabic and Islam.

Zwemer was ready to travel anywhere Muslims could be found. He was passionate about the importance of personal evangelism, and he followed a familiar pattern. He would address Muslims with the gospel by whatever available means, he would promote the publication and circulation of tracts, and he would challenge Christians to be more active in witnessing to Muslims, particularly through Bibles and other Christian literature. Alongside everything else, he kept reading, editing *The Moslem World*, and working on his next book manuscript. Amy once remarked, "Samuel never stops writing."

In 1929, Zwemer accepted the appointment to become professor of missions in Princeton Theological Seminary. He saw this as an opportunity to influence a continual stream of young men who were entering the ministry at home and abroad and to challenge them to consider missions. He remained at Princeton until his retirement at the age of seventy-one. Amy, who had shared so many of the burdens of his active life, died suddenly in 1937. A few years later his old colleague, James Cantine, introduced him to Margaret Clarke, and they were married in 1940.

Throughout his lifetime Zwemer's theology remained biblical and conservative, in the Calvinist tradition. He spoke and wrote against liberal theologies that questioned the deity of Christ and the importance of the atonement. Over and over he insisted that to be a missionary to Muslims required a strong Christology and an overpowering emphasis on the unique work of Christ in the atonement and the resurrection.

After retiring from Princeton, Zwemer taught courses at the Missionary Training Institute of the Christian and Missionary Alliance in Nyack, New York, and at Biblical Seminary in New York City. By that time, interest in missions was waning in the mainline denominations, but among conservative and evangelical churches it was gaining momentum. In his later years Zwemer was most often invited to churches and conferences that represented his evangelical convictions. On the one hand Zwemer was open to Christians of all denominational stripes, and he accepted invitations from a broad spectrum of Christian groups. But on the fundamentals of the faith he was unflinching, and no listener was ever left in doubt about Zwemer's convictions.

Shortly after Christmas in 1946, he was a keynote speaker at the first Inter-Varsity Student Foreign Missions Fellowship Convention, held in Toronto. This was the successor of the Student Volunteer conventions, in which Zwemer had played important roles earlier in his life, and the first of the now famous Urbana Conventions sponsored by Inter-Varsity Christian Fellowship and held on the campus of the University of Illinois in Urbana.

When Zwemer was eighty-three, the mission of which he was a founder celebrated its sixtieth anniversary, and Zwemer and Margaret, his second wife, were invited to attend the celebration to be held in Kuwait on the Arabian coast. After the meetings the Zwemers went to Bahrain, where Samuel and his first wife, Amy, had opened a mission station many years before. After visiting the graves of the two Zwemer daughters, Samuel said, "If we should hold our peace, these very stones would cry out for the evangelization of Arabia!"

Margaret became ill shortly after their return from Arabia and died in 1950. Two years later, after delivering three addresses in one day at a meeting of the Inter-Varsity Christian Fellowship in New York, Zwemer suffered a heart attack. On Wednesday, April 2, 1952, the heart that beat so long and hard for missions took its rest.

After a memorial service in the First Presbyterian Church in New York City, Zwemer's body was transported to Holland, Michigan, where it was buried in the only piece of ground Zwemer ever owned, the family burial plot at the Pilgrim Home cemetery, which he inherited from his father.

Samuel Zwemer was a man of deep religious piety. Of the many books he wrote, he regarded as his favorites those that in their titles praised the Lord: *The Glory of the Incarnation*, *The Glory of the Cross*, and *The Glory of the Empty Tomb*.

Zwemer's knowledge of Islam had few equals. But above all, he loved the Muslim people and longed to see them gathered to Christ. Therein lay the passion of his life and writing—that God be glorified in the winning of the Muslim world to Christ.

PART 1

ISLAM AND CHRISTIANITY

CHAPTER
1

THE MUSLIM CHRIST

C hrist has a place in Islam as one of the greater prophets, and the Koran gives precious glimpses of the Messiah's greatness. But the Koran falls short of unveiling his glorious perfection and divine majesty. Mohammed leads his followers to the portal, but he fails to open the door. A perusal of the Koran and of the traditions on the part of any sincere Muslim who tries to interpret Jesus Christ may indeed kindle the flame of curiosity but will ever leave his heart longing unsatisfied. Yet no Muslim who reads the Koran can escape forming some opinion of Jesus Christ, the son of Mary, and therefore of giving a verdict on his person and character.*

* "Koran" and "Mohammed" were common renderings of "Quran" and "Muhammad" at the time of Zwemer's writing and in the sources he quoted. Thus the older spellings are maintained here.

This chapter is intended to show what the conclusion is in the mind of the average Muslim from the accounts already given in regard to the person and character of Jesus Christ. It develops systematically the idea of the man Jesus Christ as he stands before the Muslim mind and heart. And yet it is impossible to approach the subject and use Christian terminology, because by its denials and contradictions Islam eliminates all the Christian ideas back of this terminology.

The doctrine of the person of Jesus Christ is central, determinative, and supreme in Christian theology.[1] In dealing with the person of Jesus Christ, the church throughout the centuries has taught that he was very God and very man, and to his person there have always been ascribed, according to the teaching of the Bible, the threefold office of Prophet, Priest, and King. His eternal existence as the Son of God, his wonderful humiliation as the Son of man, and his exaltation in glory are the commonplaces of theology and the comfort of all believers.

Yet no Muslim can study the person and character of Jesus Christ according to these categories. For him they do not exist. In considering the person of Jesus Christ from a Muslim standpoint, we must first, therefore, take up the subject negatively.

What Is Denied about Christ

The Muslim idea of Christ, as of God, consists not only in what is asserted of him, but also, and more emphatically, in what is denied. The Koran denies the deity and the eternal Sonship of Jesus Christ. He is a creature like Adam. "Verily, Jesus is as Adam in the sight of God. He created him of dust; he then said to him, 'Be,' and he was" (Surah 3:52). Those who assert that Jesus Christ is more than human are infidels. "The Christians say that the Messiah is the Son of God. God fight them! How they lie!" (Surah 9:30).

4

Not only is Jesus Christ a mere creature, but also he is not essential to God or to God's plans in the world. "Who can obtain anything from God if he chose to destroy the Messiah, the son of Mary, and his mother and all who are on the earth together?" (Surah 5:19).

To Muslims a consideration of the person of Jesus Christ begins by the assertion that he was only a man among men.[2] "Jesus is no more than a servant whom we favored, and proposed as an instance of divine power to the children of Israel, and, if we pleased, we could from yourself bring forth angels to succeed you on earth" (Surah 43:59).

Nothing so arouses the hostility of the Muslim mind as the statement that Jesus Christ is the Son of God. Two passages from the Koran will make especially clear how important this denial of the Trinity is as regards their doctrine of the person of Jesus. "They say the Merciful has taken to himself a son—ye have brought a monstrous thing! The heavens well-nigh burst asunder thereat, and the earth is riven and the mountains fall down broken, that they attribute to the Merciful a son! But it becomes not the Merciful to take to himself a son" (Surah 19:91–93). "Praise belongs to God, who has not taken to himself a son and has not had a partner in his kingdom, nor had a patron against such abasement" (Surah 17:112).

Whatever the Koran and tradition may state concerning Jesus Christ, his dignity, his sinlessness, or his power to work miracles, Muslims do not distinguish his person in any way as to his nature from the other prophets who came before him. The preexistence of Christ is everywhere denied, while Muslim tradition is full of stories about the Light of Mohammed, created before all things and existing before all worlds.[3] It seems incredible that Islam, while imputing to Mohammed that which he never asserted of himself, namely, preexistence, should deny this in connection with Jesus Christ.[4]

The bitter attacks of Islam on Christianity in the Muslim press nearly always find their center in the deity and the atoning work of Jesus Christ. To Christians Jesus Christ is God and man; he is Prophet, Priest, and King. To Muslims he is only human, and while they admit that he is a prophet, his kingship and his priesthood are neither understood nor admitted. Islam is a religion without a priesthood, without a clear idea of the atonement, and therefore this central thought in the work of Jesus Christ is absent from the Muslim mind. We are not surprised, therefore, that the cross is still a stumbling block to most of Mohammed's followers, as it was to Mohammed himself.

Muslim literature of every sect and every school of thought is as positive in its rejection of these distinctively Christian doctrines as is the Koran and orthodox tradition. This literature brings out the bitter antagonism that learned Muslims hold against the deity and the cross of Jesus Christ. It recognizes Jesus Christ as a prophet but refuses to recognize him as the Son of God.

A good example of this Muslim literature is this free translation[5] of the poem "A Wonderful Question for the People of the Cross."

> You who worship Jesus, I have a question for you,
>   and can you answer it?
> If Jesus was Almighty God, with power to strike terror
>   into all men,
> Why do you believe that the Jews could make him
>   endure the agony of the cross?
> And why do you believe that God died, and was
>   buried in the dust,
> And sought from his creatures a draught of water,
>   that he might quench his fiery thirst?

And that they gave him instead myrrh and vinegar,
    a nauseous mixture,
So that he threw it on the ground because he could
    not take it?
And that he died a miserable death in an agony of thirst?
And that they put on his head a crown of thorns,
So frightful that it could turn raven locks to whiteness?
And that the blood flowed down his cheeks, and
    stained his face like henna?
And that he rode on a donkey's colt to save himself
    from the toil of the journey?
You say too that Perez, son of Tamar, was his ancestor;
One who was born of incest, and the Lord will not
    receive a bastard into his assembly.
And after that will you count him God, and not be
    in grievous error?
Nay, he is only one of the creatures of God, as he
    said of himself plainly in the Book.
And if he was God as you suppose, why did he pray
    to be delivered from the torment?
And who restored his Spirit when it left his body?
And who kept the world in its state until he came
    back from the dead?
Was there a second Lord watching its affairs?
Or did he suffer it to go to destruction?
And was he crucified for some evil he had done?
Or why did he merit the punishment?
And did the Jews do well when they crucified him,
    in order that you might be saved?
Or did they do evil that you might be delivered?
An extraordinary thing!
And if you say that they did well, I ask you, why do
    you count them enemies?

And if you say they did wrong, as they crucified God,
And this is fearful sin,
I say, why was it wrong, if without it you could not
        be saved from the judgment?
And was he himself pleased with the crucifixion, or
        angry? Tell me truly.
And if you say he was pleased with it in order that he
        might atone for the fault of the repentant,
I say that Adam sinned and repented by the grace of
        God, and God forgave him (i.e., without
        atonement).
You therefore lie about your Lord: for the matter is
        plain as the Book put it;
For he fled from his cross, and wept much for himself,
And prayed to the God of heaven:
And said, "I beseech thee, save me from this trial,"
And cried, "Eli, Eli, why do you leave me this day to
        the torment?"
"And if it is possible, O my Creator, to save me,
Save me, O best of Fathers."
And this is a proof that he was only a servant of the
        Lord without doubt.
And this is proof that you lie about him,
And say what is false.
And if you say that the cross was forced on him in
        spite of himself:
Then this Almighty God is not Almighty, for he
        hung on the cross, cursed on every side, as it
        is written.
Do not blame me for thus putting the matter.
Answer my questions.
And do not fail, because silence in this is a
        disgrace to you.

> I have given you advice, and desire only that it may
>   profit you.
> For myself, I will die a firm believer in the religion
>   of Mohammed, the noblest of men,
> As I do not wish to see the horrors of the day of
>   judgment.[6]

Not on a par with this sort of popular antagonism to the doctrine of the person of Jesus Christ as held by Christians and yet equally decisive are the statements of Seyyid Ameer of Calcutta, an able apologist for Islam:

> So far as the divinity of Christ is concerned, one can almost see the legend growing. But assuming that Jesus made use of the expressions attributed to him, do they prove that he claimed to be "the only-begotten of the Father"? With all his dreams and aspirations, his mind was absolutely exempt from those pretensions which have been fixed on him by his overzealous followers. That Jesus ever maintained he was the Son of God, in the sense in which it has been construed by Christian divines and apologists, we totally deny.[7]

Here we should notice a boastful assertion common among Muslims when arguing with Christians that they honor the Lord Jesus Christ more than Christians do. After their deliberate and systematic lowering of his dignity and depreciation of all his claims and work as given in the gospel, such statements seem strange, but most workers among Muslims have been surprised and shocked to see how great is the misconception and ignorance implied in such an assertion.

What Is Admitted about Christ

So far we have considered the Muslim idea of the person
and character of our Savior negatively. We pass on to consider
what Muslims admit and believe as regards the dignity of person and the purity of character found in Jesus Christ. One
cannot help feeling that the Muslim who has carefully studied the Koran will come to the conclusion, independently of
all the commentators, that Christ is superior to Mohammed.
It is a joy to all missionaries to know that occasionally one
finds persons who come to this conclusion and in conse-
quence turn to the Gospels, led to them by the Koran.

The Rev. T. Bomford of Peshawar told of such an instance
when he noted a man from Mecca who wrote to the Bible Society Depot in Lahore asking for a New Testament in order to
learn more of the Christ mentioned in the Koran. This is just
one of many similar cases that have been recorded. There is
no better way of preaching Christ to Muslims than by beginning with the testimony of the Koran to Jesus.

First of all, Muslims admit the dignity of Christ as prophet
and apostle, with names given to him that are applied to no
other prophet and to no other apostle. Every sincere Muslim
admits the force of this argument for the unique character and
personality of Jesus Christ, although a man among men.

Nevertheless, the average Muslim does not see the force
of this argument until his attention is called to it specially, because, even though these titles are applied to Jesus Christ, he
himself is ranked with the other apostles and prophets in such
a way as to give him no special dignity of position.

Muslims are fond of quoting the text, "We make no distinction between them" (i.e., between the prophets)—Surah
2:130, 2:285, 3:78: "Say, We believe in God and what he has
sent down to us, and what has come down to Abraham and

10

Ishmael and Isaac and Jacob; and what came down to Moses and to Jesus and the prophets from their Lord. We make no distinction between any of them."

And it is remarkable that the name of Jesus is mixed up with the other prophets in the only complete list given in the Koran (Surah 6:84): "Isaac, Jacob, David, Solomon, Job, Joseph, Moses, Aaron, Zechariah, John, Jesus, Elias, Ishmael, Elisha, Jonah, Lot." To the average Muslim the Koran and tradition yield no chronological conception of the order of prophetic history, and one would not infer from the Koran necessarily that Jesus was the last of the prophets before Mohammed or the greatest.

In the second place, Muslims teach the sinlessness of Jesus Christ. And although this sinlessness does not put Jesus Christ in a class by himself, as all the prophets are sinless in the Muslim sense of that word, yet the Koran, while mentioning the sins of Adam, David, Solomon, and other prophets, leaves no doubt as regards the purity of the character of Jesus.

Mohammed himself, of course, is also considered by all Muslims as the paragon of excellence and purity, and as one who has never sinned. In regard to Jesus Christ, however, the statements of orthodox tradition are very remarkable. The prophet said, we are told, "There is no one of the sons of Adam except Mary and her son but is touched by the devil at the time of his birth, and the child makes a loud noise from the touch."[8] Here we have the doctrine of the immaculate conception not only of the Virgin Mary but also of Jesus.

We are also told:

When Mary was standing under the palm tree, the angels defended her, and when Satan tried to get her from above, they flocked above her. Then he tried to get at her from beneath, and behold, the feet of the angels protected her. And when he tried to get in between them, they prevented him. So Satan went back and said, There is nothing ever born which was defended against me so successfully as this birth.[9]

One of the commentators, Er-Razi, says that Jesus was given the title *Messiah* "because he was kept clear from the taint of sin." There is a remarkable tradition related by Anas, which seems by implication to prove that while Mohammed admitted his own sinfulness, he could not charge Jesus with sin. Mohammed himself wrote:

In the day of resurrection Muslims will not be able to move, and they will be greatly distressed, and will say, "Would to God that we had asked him to create someone to intercede for us, that we might be taken from this place and be delivered from tribulation and sorrow."

Then these men will go to Adam and will say, "Thou art the father of all men, God created thee with his hand, and made thee a dweller in Paradise, and ordered his angels to prostrate themselves before thee, and taught thee the names of all things. Ask grace for us, we pray thee!"

And Adam will say, "I am not of that degree of eminence you suppose, for I committed a sin in eating of the grain which was forbidden. Go to Noah, the prophet, he was the first who was sent by God to go to the unbelievers on the face of the earth."

Then they will go to Noah and ask for intercession, and he will say, "I am not of that degree which ye suppose." And he will remember the sin which he committed in asking for the deliverance of his son (Hud), not knowing whether it was a right request or not; and he will say, "Go to Abraham, who is the friend of God."

Then they will go to Abraham, and he will say, "I am not of that degree which ye suppose." And he will remember the three occasions on which he told lies in the world; and he will say, "Go to Moses, who is the servant whom God gave his law, and whom he allowed to converse with him."

And they will go to Moses, and Moses will say, "I am not of that degree which ye suppose." And he will remember the sin which he committed in slaying a man, and he will say, "Go to Jesus, he is the servant of God, the apostle of God, the Spirit of God, and the Word of God."

Then they will go to Jesus, and he will say, "Go to Mohammed who is a servant, whose sins God has forgiven both first and last." Then the Muslims will come to me, and I will then ask permission to go into God's presence and intercede for them.[10]

There is also this curious version of the temptation of Jesus that may indicate his victory over the devil but is not very conclusive. Taus of Yemen, one of the early followers of Mohammed, used to say, "There is nothing which a man says but is counted against him, even his moaning in illness."

He went on to say:

Jesus having met Iblis, the latter said to him, "Do you not know that nothing will betide you but what is destined for you?" Jesus replied, "Yes." Iblis then said, "Ascend to the summit of this mountain and throw yourself down, see whether you will live or not." Jesus replied, "Do you not know that God has said, 'My ser-

13

vant cannot test me, for I do what I please?' Verily, a servant does not try his Lord, but God tries His servant." . . . Iblis therefore became his enemy.[11]

In the third place, Jesus Christ is the great Miracle Worker, especially as the healer of the sick. It is the common opinion among Muslims that the science of medicine had reached a high degree of perfection in the days of Jesus Christ and that God glorified his apostle by making it possible for him to heal the sick through miraculous power. We have seen in the story of the miracles of Jesus how this conception is elaborated. Jesus Christ as the Great Physician is a familiar picture to Muslims.

The following beautiful account of Jesus healing the sick occurs in the *Masnavi*[12] and may well compare with our evening hymn, "At evening, ere the sun was set, the sick, O Lord, around thee lay."

> The house of 'Isa was the banquet of men of heart,
> Ho! afflicted one, quit not this door!
> From all sides the people ever thronged,
> Many blind and lame, and halt and afflicted,
> To the door of the house of 'Isa at dawn,
> That with his breath he might heal their ailments.
> As soon as he had finished his orisons,
> That holy one would come forth at the third hour;
> He viewed those impotent folk, troop by troop,
> Sitting at his door in hope and expectation;
> He spoke to them, saying, "O stricken ones!
> The desires of all of you have been granted by God!
> Arise, walk without pain or affliction,
> Acknowledge the mercy and beneficence of God!"
> Then all, as camels whose feet are shackled,

When you loose their feet in the road,
Straightway rush in joy and delight to the halting
     place,
So did they run upon their feet at his command.

Lastly, Christ is alive and in heaven, where he is able to
intercede for his people. In his commentary on the text in the
Koran where it says of Christ that he is "illustrious in this
world and the next" (Surah 3:46), Zamakhshari says, "This
signifies the office of prophet and supremacy over men in this
world, and in the next world the office of Intercessor and lofti-
ness of rank in Paradise."

Muslims disagree as to where Jesus Christ now is. The
Sunni divines agree that he saw no corruption, but they differ
as to the exact state of celestial bliss in which he now resides
in his human body. Some say he is in the second heaven;
some say he is in the third; some say the fourth.[13] A learned
doctor of the Shiah sect assured me that the Shiah belief is
that he is in the highest, or the seventh, heaven.

Gathering up these ideas of the character of Jesus and his
person, and yet remembering what they deny in regard to our
Savior, it is evident that to Muslims the Founder of the Christian religion, although miraculously born, with power to work
miracles, and the last and greatest of all the prophets until
Mohammed, who also had the special honor of being taken
up into heaven, is nevertheless a mere man, sent of God, and
one of the objects of his mission (and this is always the climax
of Muslim teaching) was that Jesus came to announce the
coming of Mohammed.

This idea has taken a permanent and prominent place in
all later Muslim teaching concerning the person of Jesus and
is often the first argument on Muslim lips. Every Muslim,
even boys who are well read in their religion, can glibly quote

Surah 61:6: "And remember when Jesus the son of Mary said, 'O children of Israel! of a truth I am God's apostle to you to confirm the law which was given before me, and to announce an apostle that shall come after me, whose name shall be Ahmed.'" By this token from the lips of Mohammed himself and alleged to be a revelation from God, the prophet of Arabia not only succeeds but supplants the Prophet of Nazareth.

Muslims have always been eager to find further proof of the coming of Mohammed in the Old and New Testament Scriptures in addition to their misinterpretation of John 16:7, regarding the Paraclete.[14] They therefore not only quote the words of the Koran but also refer to Deuteronomy 33:2, Isaiah 21:6, and the parable in Matthew 20, John 4:21, and 1 John 4:1–3.

The passage in Deuteronomy states that Jehovah came from Sinai and rose from Seir unto them; he shined forth from Mount Paran. Sinai is a Jewish mountain; Seir, they say, is a mountain in Galilee where Christ died. Paran, however, is a mountain near Mecca and signifies the Muslim religion.

As for Isaiah's prophecy in which he sees an approaching troop of horsemen and of men riding asses and of others riding camels, to which the prophet should hearken diligently, their interpretation is that the horses refer to Moses' dispensation, the asses to Christ's arrival (in that he rode one), and the camels to Mohammed's coming.

The parable of the laborers in the vineyard in the twentieth chapter of Matthew's Gospel is cleverly applied to the threefold dispensation: the morning, Judaism; the noonday laborers, the apostles of Christ; and those to whom he came in the evening, the Muslims. This interpretation is based on a most interesting statement attributed to Mohammed in the traditions:

Your likeness, O Muslims, in comparison to the Jews and Christians, is like that of a man who hired laborers. He said, "Who will work for me a whole day for a shekel?" These are the Jews, for they have labored a long time for a small wage. Then said the man, "Who will work from noon until night for a shekel?" These are the Christians. Then he said, "Who will work from afternoon prayer time until sunset?" Such laborers are ye, and remember that for you there is a double wage, because ye have acknowledged the prophet of Truth, and in him all the other prophets.

The tradition goes on to show how the Jews and Christians complained, in the terms of the parable, and how God said, "I will give those whom I love what I will."[15]

According to John 4:21, the true worshipers of God are those who "neither on this mountain nor in Jerusalem" worship him, meaning that Muslims are the true worshipers of God.

The most daring use of Scripture, however, as a prophecy of the coming of Mohammed, is the Muslim interpretation of the last passage mentioned. "Hereby know ye the Spirit of God. Every spirit that confesseth that Jesus Christ is come in the flesh is of God." Mohammed is the true Spirit of God because he taught that Jesus Christ was come in the flesh; namely, he came as man and man only, not as God.[16]

After this fashion the Koran and its interpreters unite to obscure the glory of the person and character of Jesus Christ, by obtruding Mohammed as the last of the prophets and the one to whom even Jesus Christ bears witness.

CHAPTER

2

MOHAMMED
AND CHRIST

As in a total eclipse of the sun the glory and the beauty of the heavenly orb are hidden and only the corona appears on the edge, so in the life and thought of Muslims their own prophet has almost eclipsed Jesus Christ. The general idea of his life, as we have gathered it from many Muslim sources, is, after all, vague, shadowy, and not at all clearly outlined in the mind of Muslims. An Arab from Hassa expressed this truth when he said to me, "Until my wife became a Christian, I knew nothing of Jesus whatever—only his name and that he was a prophet!"

Whatever place Jesus Christ may occupy in the Koran—and the portrait there given is a sad caricature—whatever favorable critics may say about Christ's honorable place among the Muslim prophets, it is nevertheless true that the large bulk of Muslims know extremely little, and think still less, of Jesus

19

Christ. He has no place in their hearts or in their lives. All the prophets have not only been succeeded but supplanted by Mohammed; he is at once the sealer and concealer of all former revelations. Mohammed is always in the foreground, and Jesus Christ, in spite of his lofty titles and the honor given him in the Koran, is in the background. Christ is grouped with the other prophets, with Lot, Alexander the Great, Ishmael, Moses, Abraham, and Adam.

We cannot forget this fact when we try to form a conception of the Muslim Christ. It is because of this that Islam presents difficulties offered by no other religion in the work of missions. "It cannot be treated like any other religion," says Rev. W. H. T. Gairdner.

> It baffles more than any other, for it is more difficult to concede to it what is gladly conceded to other religions that appeared before Christ, that they in some part prepared and prepare the way for Him. How can that which denies the whole essential and particular content of the message be said to prepare for Him, or to be a half-way house to His kingdom? That is what Islam does. Other religions know nothing of Christianity; one and all they came before it, and speak of it neither good nor evil. But the whole theory of Islam is that it, the latest sent of all religions, does not so much abrogate Christianity with its Book, as specifically and categorically deny both as willful corruption and lies.[1]

The sin and the guilt of the Muslim world is that they give Christ's glory to another, and that for all practical purposes Mohammed himself is the Muslim Christ. The life and character of Mohammed as portrayed for us by his earliest biographers, who were all his faithful followers and admirers, leaves no doubt that he was thoroughly human and liable to error. Later tradition had changed all this and made him sinless and almost divine.

The two hundred and one titles of honor given to Mohammed proclaim his apotheosis. These names and titles are current in all popular books of devotion among Muslims. From Morocco to China they are separately printed and learned by heart in Muslim schools. The list that follows contains at least two score of names that Christians would apply only to Christ, and many of them are by Muslims themselves applied to God as well as to their prophet, namely,

Mohammed, Ahmed, Hamid, Mahmood, the Unique, The Only, *The Forgiver*, the Raiser of the Dead, The Avenger, "Ta Ha," "Ya Seen,"[2] The Pure, The Purified, The Good, The Lord, The Apostle, The Prophet,[3] The Apostle of Mercy, The Manager, The Gatherer, The Follower, The Leader, The Apostle of War, The Apostle of Rest, *The Perfect*, The Crown, The Wrapped One, The Covered One, Servant of God, Beloved of God, Chosen of God, Companion of God, Mouthpiece of God, Seal of Prophets, Seal of Apostles, *The Quickener*, The Deliverer, The Reminder, The Victorious, The Victor, Prophet of Mercy, Prophet of Repentance, *The Watcher*, The Well-known, The Famous, The Witness, The Martyr, The Witnessed, Bringer of Good Tidings, The Preacher, The One under Vows, The Warner, *The Light*, The Lamp, The Candle, The Guidance, *The Guide*, The Mahdi, The Enlightener, The Summoner, The Called One, *The Answerer of Prayer*, *The Interceder*, The Hidden, *The Pardoner*, The Saint, *The*

Truth, *The Strong*, *The Faithful*, The Entrusted One, *The Gracious*, The Honored, The Valiant, The Mighty, The Evident, *The Mediator*, The Bestower, The Able, The Honorable, The Exalted, The Possessor of Might, The Possessor of Grace, The Obedient, The Subjector, The Benevolent, *The Merciful*, The Good Tidings, The Assister, The Provider, *The Benefactor*, The Mercy of God, The Straight Way, The Memorial of God, The Sword of God, The Portion of God, The Shining Star, The Exalted, The Corrector of Evil, The Bearer of Faults, The Illiterate, The Chosen One, The Rewarded, The Mighty One, Abu Kasim, Abu Tahir, Abu Tayyib, Aby Ibrahim, The Intercessor, The Interceder, The Pious, The Peace Maker, The Guarder, The Truthful, The Upright, *Verity*, Lord of Apostles, Leader of the Pious, Leader of Pure Women, Friend of the Merciful, *Righteousness*, *The Justifier*, The Illustrious, The Adviser, The Man of Counsel, The Undertaker, The Entrusted, The Surety, *The Compassionate*, The Founder of the Law, *The Holy One, Holy Spirit, The Spirit of Truth*, The Spirit of Rectitude, The All-Sufficient, The Sufficer, The Perfect One, The One Who Attained, The Healer, The Giver, The Gift, The Forerunner, The Rear Guard, The Rightly Guided, The Right Guidance, *The Beginner*, The Precious, The Honored, The Honor-laden, *The Opener*, The Key, The Key of Mercy, the Key of Paradise, The Source of Faith, *The Source of Truth*, The Guide to Plenty, The Selected One, The Purifier of Good Works, *The Pardoner of Sins*, The Lord of Intercession, The Highly Exalted, The Most Noble, The Essence of Power, The Essence of Glory, The Essence of Honor, The One Who

Helps, The One Who Has a Sword, The One Who
Has Praise, The One Who Has a Covering, The Argument, The Sultan, The Possessor of the Cloak, The
Possessor of High Degree, The Possessor of the Crown,
The Possessor of the Helmet, The Possessor of the Ban-
ner, One Who Ascended to Heaven, The Possessor of
the Scepter, The Possessor of the Seal, The Possessor
of Boraak,[4] The Possessor of the Sign, The Possessor of
the Proof, The Possessor of the Argument, The Elo-
quent, The Pure of Heart, *The Gracious One, The Piti-
ful*, The Ear of Goodness, The Perfection of Islam,
Lord of Two Worlds, The Eye of Kindness, The Eye of
Brilliancy, The Helper of God, The Helper of Men,
The Pleader for the Nations, The Knowledge of Truth,
The Discloser of Secrets, The Elevator of the Lowly,
The Glory of the Arabs, The One Who Has Victory.

Some of these titles, as we have indicated by printing
them in italics, are similar to those given to God himself. Mohammed is also called the Light of God, the Peace of the
World, the Glory of the Ages, the First of All Creatures, and
other names of yet greater import. One tradition goes so far as
to say, "No man in whatsoever condition he is can resemble
God so much as thou dost. But if there could be an image to
represent God as he is, it could be no other than thyself."[5]

No Muslim prays to Mohammed, but every Muslim prays
for him in endless repetition daily. In spite of statements in
the Koran to the contrary, most Muslims believe that he will
be the only intercessor on the day of judgment. The books of
devotion used everywhere are proof of this statement. God favored him above all creatures; he dwells in the highest heaven
and is several degrees above Jesus in honor and station. Mohammed holds the keys of heaven and hell: no Muslim, how-

ever bad his character, will perish finally; no unbeliever, however good his life, can be saved except through Mohammed.

Islam denies the need of Christ as Mediator, only to substitute Mohammed as a mediator, without an incarnation, without an atonement, and without demand for a change of character. One has only to question the Muslim masses or to read tradition in proof of these statements.[6]

Every detail of the life of Jesus Christ has been imitated and parodied by Mohammed's later biographers and admirers.

As it developed, Muslim theology, quite aware of Christianity, sought increasingly to link Jesus and the founder of Islam, and to attribute to Mohammed miracles which helped make him at least an equal of Jesus. This deviation from the actual image which people had of the prophet started early on and increased over time. The miracles are a carbon copy of those reported in the gospels and, as a matter of fact, stand in complete opposition to the actual sentiments of Mohammed himself.[7]

Muslim authors attribute to their prophet an equality with, and even a superiority to, the Prophet of Nazareth, by ascribing to him all the glory that centers on the Christ in the New Testament. Preexistence is ascribed to Mohammed, and his genealogy is traced through Abraham to Adam, as in the case of Jesus Christ. An angel announced Mohammed's conception and birth and the name that he was to bear. Mohammed, like Jesus, was lost in his childhood and found again, and at the age of twelve he took a special journey. After the commencement of his public ministry Mohammed, like Jesus, passed through a remarkable ordeal of satanic temptation. Mohammed, like Jesus Christ, chose twelve apostles. His enemies were those of his own household, and he was recognized by spirits from the unseen world more readily than by those to whom he was sent. The demons knew Jesus; the jinn accepted Islam at the hands of Mohammed. The transfiguration of Jesus Christ is surpassed by the story of Mohammed's ascent into heaven, where he had personal communion with all the previous prophets, and leaving Jesus far below in the second heaven, himself mounted to the seventh, where, according to Muslim tradition, he ate and drank with God.

Traditions show that, as Jesus Christ is to us, so Mohammed is to Muslims above all other men in worth and dignity. He was the greatest and best of all God's messengers; his body the true temple in which the divine Presence dwelt. Mohammed bore the divine seal of prophecy and imparted divine benefits by laying on his hands. As a parody of the mystery of the Lord's Supper, Mohammed is said to have sanctioned the drinking of his own blood. When Malik bin Sinan sucked his wounds, swallowing the blood, the prophet exclaimed, "Anyone whose blood touches mine, him the fire of hell shall not destroy."

The miracles of Jesus Christ, even the fantastic miracles ascribed to him by Muslim tradition, shrink into insignificance compared with the miracles ascribed to Mohammed by tradition. Feeding a hungry multitude with a handful of dates, opening the eyes of the blind, healing the sick, turning barren lands into fruitful fields, and raising the dead—all these and many other things are attributed to Mohammed.[8]

In his death as well as in his life Mohammed is made to resemble Jesus Christ. His death was foretold; it was not unavoidable but freely accepted by him; he died a martyr's death, and his sufferings were meritorious, taking away sin and helping those who believe in him to enter paradise. Not only are all these superhuman characteristics and divine glories ascribed to Mohammed in tradition, but also he is the prophet to whom all former prophets bore witness and concerning whose coming they testified.

Jesus Christ is supplanted by Mohammed not only in Muslim tradition and in the hearts of the common people. He is supplanted in the hearts of all Muslims by Mohammed. They are jealous for his glory and resist any attempt to magnify the glory of Jesus Christ at the expense of Mohammed.

In the Gospel of Barnabas, a spurious document dating about the middle of the sixteenth century and not referred to by Muslims until after Sale had called attention to it in his translation of the Koran, Mohammed is also called the Messiah. The Gospel of Barnabas was evidently written by a Christian renegade in the Middle Ages and has for its special object the advancement of Islam, the author desiring to foist upon the world a forgery that would strengthen the claims of Mohammed and prove that Jesus Christ had foretold his coming. Every reader of the Koran knows that Jesus Christ is spoken of consistently in that book as the Messiah, yet, strange to say, this Gospel of Barnabas again and again gives Mohammed that title, while Jesus is made his forerunner, as John the Baptist was to Christ in the canonical Gospels.

Although this Gospel of Barnabas is evidently a late forgery, it is used by Muslims as an argument against Christianity. This shows how, with the centuries, Mohammed had gradually taken the place of Jesus Christ in Muslim literature, and how even his supreme title of the Christ, or the Messiah, has, both in the Middle Ages and in current periodical literature, been given to the prophet of Arabia.[9] Whether the title of Messiah is given him or not, Mohammed is for all practical purposes the Muslim Christ.

Islam is indeed the only anti-Christian religion. This world faith takes issue with everything that is vital in the

Christian religion, because it takes issue in its attitude toward the Christ. By this it must stand or fall.

In this respect all schools of Muslim thought are practically the same. They differ in ritual and tradition; in interpretations, broad or narrow; in going back to the old Koran or in advocating the new Islam; but whether Shiahs or Sunnis, Wahabis or followers of Seyyid Ameer Ali, their position as regards the Christ is practically the same.[10]

Islam is not a preparation for Christianity; it is easier to build on a strange soil than first of all to tear down old buildings that are so firmly set together that they offer an insurmountable obstacle to demolition.[11]

Christianity gladly admits the strength of theism. We assert as strongly as do all Muslims that there is only one God, but because there is only one God there can be only one gospel and one Christ. Dr. James Denney, in his book *The Death of Christ*, says, "It pleased the Father" that in Jesus Christ "all fullness should dwell," not in Mohammed (Col. 1:19). "In him dwelleth all the fullness of the Godhead bodily," not in Mohammed (Col. 2:9). "In [him] are hid all the treasures of wisdom and knowledge," not in Mohammed (Col. 2:3). He is "the way, the truth, and the life," not Mohammed (John 14:6). This is the issue that cannot be avoided.

The only Christianity that has a missionary message for the Muslim world is this vital Christianity. It is the only Christianity that can meet the deepest need of our Muslim brothers. Our love for them is only increased by our intolerance of their rejection of the Christ; we cannot bear it, it pains us. The day is coming when many will confess him in the words of a Muslim convert to a Christian woman who was visiting her: "I see now that the very center of your religion is Christ, and I want to love and serve him."

The main question is the old question, "What think ye of Christ?" (Matt. 22:42).

CHAPTER

3

ornament

ISLAM AND THE
HOLY SPIRIT

I f the cross is to triumph over the crescent it will be not by might or by power but by God's Spirit. The Crusades were a colossal error on the part of Christendom. They showed zeal but without knowledge, passion without the love of Christ. Our hope for missions is based on our faith in the Holy Spirit, the Lord and Giver of life. It is also strengthened by the promises of God in the Old Testament regarding Arabia and the Arabs—a sure word of prophecy, to which we do well to take heed as to a light shining in a dark place. It is to these two that we turn our attention in this chapter.

The Holy Spirit and Islam

But why speak of the Holy Spirit and Islam? Is there not an incongruity in this juxtaposition of two words? Did the

Holy Spirit also speak through him whom our Muslim brethren designate as the last and greatest of the prophets? Can there be relation between the Dove of Peace and the Sword of Islam? Historically, ethically, and spiritually the upper room in Jerusalem and the prophet's chamber in Medina seem as far apart as the East is from West, Averroes from Newton, Harum from Alfred, 'Aisha from Mary Magdalene, 'Ali from St. Paul, Bethlehem's manger from the Kaaba at Mecca. And yet our very confession that the Holy Spirit is "the Lord and Giver of life" — of all life and the only source of life — compels us to think more deeply and with truer judgment on this relationship.

The rigid monotheism of Islam has no true place for the doctrine of the Holy Spirit. The words "holy spirit" occur only four times in the Koran and are of very doubtful significance. Some say that the Holy Spirit is Gabriel, the angel of revelation; others identify the term with breath, light, prophecy, the Koran, or God's great name. Yet we gather from orthodox Muslim interpretation that although shrouded in mystery, "the Spirit" proceeds from God, is limitless, and can be infused into countless personalities. It was breathed into Adam and into the Virgin Mary at the birth of Jesus. But all this is still removed from the Christian idea of the Holy Spirit.

The late Temple Gairdner loved to speculate on the Muslim doctrine of the Spirit as a possible point of contact with Muslims in preaching to them the unsearchable riches of Christ. He saw how near Mohammed came to the mystery and yet how far off he remained. In his paper for the Jerusalem council meeting, Gairdner wrote:

> If Mohammed's awful Visitant was none other than the Spirit, then the Spirit was a being altogether higher than the angels, for he describes the Spirit as "endued with power, having influence with the Lord

of the Throne, obeyed" (by celestials, surely). There results the noblest and most convincing interpretation attempted by Islamic thinkers, namely: the Spirit is a unique Being, above all creatures, related uniquely, intimately, and actively to the Lord of the throne.

This teaching, though rare, and to the multitude unknown, and even for adepts full of awesome and dangerous mystery, is a part of what Christ came not to destroy but to fulfill. It seems clear that Muslim theologians, though following the way to truth, wavered when within a step of their goal, out of respect for their commendable belief in the unity of the Deity. They saw the transcendental character of the Spirit, even admitted (some of them) that the Spirit is uncreated, but hesitated to admit the Spirit's eternity. In many of his attributes, the Spirit of whom the Koran speaks is the Holy Spirit of the Bible, or at least of the Old Testament, in all but name.

Some would hesitate to endorse all of this statement. For in this connection we must not forget that among the titles given to Mohammed is that of Paraclete! Muslim writers assert that Christ in his last discourse foretold the coming of the prophet and that the Greek word translated Paraclete (originally, they say, Pariclite), signified Mohammed. This error arose early and is commonly believed among all classes of Muslims. It has been answered again and again by Christian apologists but persists in many popular Islamic tracts and books to this day.

On the other hand, no one can read the writings of the Mohammedan mystics without being convinced that God's Spirit led them toward and not away from the light and the truth.

Ghazali's testimony to the character and sinlessness of Jesus Christ, All-Sha'rani's ingenious and reverent speculation on why Jesus is called the Spirit of God, and the words of the *Masnavi* are instances in point:

> For granite man's heart is, till grace intervene
> And, crushing it, clothe the long barren with green;
> When the fresh breath [Spirit] of Jesus shall touch
>   the heart's core
> It will live, it will breathe, it will blossom once more.

Whatever may be the doctrine of the Holy Spirit in Islam, we know that for those in contact with Islam, as missionaries, every virtue these witnesses (theologians, Sufis, and pious folk) possess, every victory won, every thought of holiness, every deed of kindness, every ministry of love, is his alone. It is God's common grace that enabled them, as even Calvin taught.

Moreover, whatever values lie hidden in the non-Christian religions come directly or indirectly through the witness and work of the Spirit. For the Reformed theology has always spoken of common as well as of special grace. By the former, Calvin meant those gracious influences or restraints of the Holy Spirit exercised in the natural heart of fallen man and throughout the history of the race, by which the soil was prepared for the seed of the Word and by which human hearts were made to yearn for God. God's creative image was disfigured by the fall, but not wholly lost.

Here is an illustration from my experience. One morning, many years ago, sailing on the Indian Ocean, we read, with a Muslim, a little manual of daily devotion published at Colombo, in Tamil and Arabic. It was a book of prayers of the Naqshbandi dervishes and is typical of this kind of literature, which is everywhere in the hands and on the lips of the people. Here is a translation of one beautiful page:

I am truly bankrupt. O God, I stand before the door of thy riches. Truly I have great sins—forgive me for thine own sake. Truly I am a stranger, a sinner, a humble slave who has nothing but forgetfulness and disobedience to present to thee. My sins are as the sands, without number. Forgive me and pardon me. Remove my transgressions and undertake my cause. Truly my heart is sick, but thou art able to heal it. My condition, O God, is such that I have no good work. My evil deeds are many, and my provision of obedience is small. Speak to the fire of my heart, as thou didst in the case of Abraham, "be cool for my servant."

The reference here is to a story in the Koran of Abraham's trial by fire. What do you make of such prayers for pardon?

The witness to Christ in the Koran, the spiritual poetry and prayers of the mystics, the present-day admiration for the character of Jesus, the desire to search the Holy Scriptures, the friendliness and sympathy where formerly there was hostility and fanaticism—all these surely are the work of God's Spirit. Yet this is only preparatory to his work of conversion and should urge us to prayer for an outpouring of God's Spirit. Apart from him we can do nothing. If our stupendous spiritual task meets with success anywhere and in any way, it is not by might nor by power but by the Holy Spirit alone. The Holy Spirit is the one and only source of all true power for evangelism.

The Promises of God

The Holy Spirit spoke by the prophets. In the Old Testament Scriptures the promises of God to Ishmael and his descendants and the spread of the Messiah's kingdom across the Arabian Peninsula have been too long neglected. In his book,

Arabia and the Bible, Professor J. A. Montgomery calls attention to the prominence of the Arab in the Old Testament. An
index of all the scriptural references to Arabia and the Arabian
Bedouin life includes twenty-five books of the Old Testament
and five of the New. The messianic promises in the Psalms
and in Isaiah group themselves around seven names that have
from of old been identified with Arabia—Ishmael, Kedar,
Nebaioth, Sheba, Seba, Midian, and Ephah.

Hagar is not referred to in the Koran by name, although,
Ishmael, her son is mentioned several times. In Surah 4:161
of the Koran it is said of him that he received revelations; in
19:55 he is called a messenger and a prophet; and in 2:119 he
along with Abraham is commanded to purify the holy house
at Mecca.

The traditions are more explicit. According to the strange
Muslim story, Ishmael helped his father, Abraham, build the
temple at Mecca. When the work was completed, Abraham
abandoned the boy with his mother in a barren country. Af-
flicted by thirst, Hagar ran to and fro between the hills al-Safa
and al-Marwa looking for water. Gabriel called to her, and the
result was the spring of Zamzam. The sacred waters of this
miraculous spring are now used by all the pilgrims at Mecca.

According to genealogies, Ishmael is considered the ancestor of the North Arabian tribes. Muslim tradition also notes
the story related in Genesis 22; but here Ishmael, and not
Isaac, is offered on the altar and delivered by God's providing
a ram. With knowledge of these Arab traditions, Isaac Da
Costa, the Dutch poet, wrote one of the finest missionary poems in the world of literature. Soon after his conversion to
Christianity this cultured Jew became the uncrowned poet
laureate of the Netherlands. Of all his poems, perhaps "Hagar" is the most oriental, and that is saying much in the case
of the poet who said of himself:

I'm not a son of lukewarm Western lands,
My fatherland is where the sun awakens;
And like the warming glow of Libyan sands
Is the thirst for poetry that casts its beams upon me.

The poem, "Hagar," appears in the third volume of his complete works (137–48) and consists of 340 lines. It was first published in 1855 in a small collection entitled *Hesperiden: Bijbelsche Vrouwen* (Women of the Bible).

Not only is the poem oriental but, strictly speaking, Arabian from beginning to end. The scene opens in the desert, with a vision of Hagar at the well. It tells the tale of her desert son and his descendants and closes with a last vision of the mother of sorrow — Sarah's bondmaid.

In 168 rhymed couplets the genius of Da Costa has condensed the story of Ishmael and Islam in their origin and development. He has woven together the woof of Bible promise and the warp of Arabian history into one beautiful seamless garment of poetry. To give a worthy rendering of the whole, or even of some lofty stanzas, would be hopeless. Parts of the poem yield to a sort of rendering in English, which may, perhaps, be called a translation. At least, they are as literal as I could make them while adhering to the measure, form, and stanzas of the original. Addressing Arabia, the poem opens:

What marvels met thine eye, thou Orient desert queen!
Eternal land of drought, of crags and rocks between
A shifty sea of sand, vast, limitless . . .
A sea of solitude, oppressive, comfortless. . . .
Whose waves of sand and rock refresh no aching eye,
But leave earth barren 'neath a burning sky.
How oft beneath those skies the storm winds thou
        hast seen.

Fiercer than oven blast, hotter than midday beam,
Chainlike unfolding in their onward path,
Whilst knelt the caravan obedient to their wrath;
Until, storm-built and driven by the blast,
The simoon's awful chariot had rolled past.
. . . .
But in the solemn hour, recalled by poet's muse,
Silent the desert wastes. The rushing storm winds lose
Their faintest whisper. Solitude.
Save one! With bold, yet downcast eye, a woman
        walks alone.
Sorrow hath filled her soul.

Then follows the vision of Hagar and the promise of Jehovah. The second part tells of Ishmael's mocking, the exile,
Hagar's prayer, and the renewed promise of God to her seed:

Ishmael, thou shalt not die: The desert waste,
Which dared to boast itself thy grave, shall taste
And tell thy glory.

Here the Bedouin life is sketched in a few matchless stanzas portraying the ship of the desert and the Arabian steed—
the peculiar twofold treasure of the peninsula from time
immemorial.

Passing by the centuries of silence, the poet suddenly
places before us the Saracen invasion and its onward sweep
into North Africa and Spain:

They leap upon the lance, but lances wound them not;
A hemisphere at once falls to the Arab's lot.
And, as a new-plowed field sown thick with summer hail
Pressed from the thunder could, so swift their nomad trail

Sweeps everywhere along. . . .
The day of vengeance falls! The Koran and its sword!
Those half-truths, wrapped in fascinating lore,
Your idols can confound but not your God restore.
Yet conquer must that Christendom which sold
Her substance for a form; for glitter lost her gold,
And thus waxed weak. Egypt, once more obey
The nomad's law, like Hyksos rule in earlier day!
Proud Alexandria, bow! Yield, yield thy costly store.
Thy libraries of learning and their treasured lore,
With all thy boasted schools? The latest blood
Of old Numidia now lies reeking on the sod,
Nor Carthager, nor Vandal, can ward off the blow. . . .
All Africa's at stake, and Europe shares her woe.
They've mounted high Gibraltar, lovely Spain
Lies just beyond . . . 'tis Christian but in name;
The fierce West-Goth sees all his temples sacked
Till turns the tide of time by greater Power backed.
Alas! Still ebbs the flood. No Pyrenees can bar
The eagle's lofty flight nor stay the scimitar.
Awake, ye north winds, and drive back the horde
Barbarian; Karel, rise, thou Marel, break their sword!
God's hand makes true thy name. Regain our loss
And save from crescent rule the lands that love the
      cross. . . .

Next, we have in the poem a full-length portrait of the genius prophet, Mohammed, the greatest of the sons of Hagar. These stanzas defy translation because of their beauty and idiom and marvelous condensation. There is often a volume of thought in a single line, and nowhere do I know of a more just, generous, and yet critically truthful delineation of Mohammed's character.

The seventh division of the poem opens, as do all the others, by addressing Hagar, but this time as the bondmaid; Ishmael in subjection to Isaac; the cross rising triumphant above the crescent:

Mother of Ishmael! The word that God hath spoken
Never hath failed the least, nor was his promise broken.
Whether in judgment threatened or as blessing given;
Whether for time and earth or for eternal heaven,
To Esau or to Jacob. . . .
The patriarch prayed to God, while bowing in the dust:
"O that before thee Ishmael might live!"—his prayer,
       his trust.
Nor was that prayer despised, that promise left alone
Without fulfillment. For the days shall come
When Ishmael shall bow his haughty, chieftain head
Before that greatest Chief of Isaac's royal seed.
Thou, favored Solomon, hast first fulfillment seen
Of Hagar's promise, when came suppliant Sheba's
      queen.
Next Araby the blest brought Bethlehem's new-
      born King,
Her myrrh and spices, gold and offering.
Again at Pentecost they came, first fruits of harvest vast;
When, to adore the name of Jesus, at the last
To Zion's glorious hill the nation's joy to share
The scattered flocks of Kedar all are gathered there,
Nebajoth, Hefa, Midian. . . .
Then Israel shall know Whose heart their hardness
      broke,
Whose side they pierced, Whose curse they dared
      invoke.
And then, while at his feet they mourn his bitter death,

Receive his pardon. . . .
Before whose same white throne Gentile and Jew
        shall meet
With Parthian, Roman, Greek, the far North and the
        South,
From Mississippi's source to Ganges' giant mouth,
And every tongue and tribe shall join in one new song,
Redemption! Peace on earth, and good will unto men;
The purpose of all ages unto all ages sure. Amen.
Glory unto the Father! Glory the Lamb, once slain,
Spotless for human guilt, exalted now to reign!
And to the Holy Ghost, Life-giver, whose refreshing
Makes all earth's deserts bloom with living showers
        of blessing!

. . . .

Mother of Ishmael! I see thee yet once more,
Thee, under burning skies and on a waveless shore!
Thou comfortless, soul storm-tossed, tempest-shaken,
Heart full of anguish and of hope forsaken,
Thou, too, didst find at last God's glory all thy stay!
He came. He spoke to thee. He made thy night his day.
As then, so now. Return to Sarah's tent
And Abraham's God, and better covenant,
And sing with Mary, through her Savior free,
"God of my life, thou hast looked down on me."

CHRISTIANITY'S STUMBLING BLOCK

Throughout the New Testament the cross dominates everything. It interprets everything and puts all things in their true relations to each other. The death of Christ is the central truth in the New Testament, and therefore, as James Denny remarks, "both for the propagation and for the scientific construction of the Christian religion, the death of Christ is of supreme importance." How is this fact related to the Muslim problem? Is the death of Christ and his atoning work our supreme message? Ought it to be our first message?

The fundamental difference between Islam and Christianity is the absence in the former of the doctrine of the cross. The cross of Christ is the missing link in the Muslim's creed, and not only in the Koran and in the early traditions, but in the practical experience of every missionary. Especially in lands that are wholly Muslim, nothing seems to stand out more prominently than Islam's hatred of the cross. The Koran gives Jesus Christ a high place among the prophets and confers on him names and titles that, if rightly interpreted, would place him above them all, and yet it does so only by denying his death and his atonement.

Modern Islam differs in no respect from orthodox Islam in this particular, and although the followers of the new Islam may speak in the highest terms of Jesus Christ as regards his character, his miracles, and his influence on history, they maintain the orthodox position in this respect. Nor do they find a place in their doctrine of salvation for Christ's atonement. A recent writer, and a missionary of long experience, goes so far as to say that there is "not a single important fact in the life, person, and work of our Savior which is not ignored, perverted, or denied by Islam." Their chief denial, however, is of his death.

There are three passages in the Koran which seem to indicate that Christ did die:

> But they [the Jews] were crafty, and God was crafty, for God is the best of crafty ones! When God said, "O Jesus! I will make thee die and take thee up again to me, and will clear thee of those who misbelieve, and will make those who follow thee above those who misbelieve, at the day of judgment, then to me is your return. I will decide between you concerning that wherein ye disagree. And as for those who misbelieve, I will punish them with grievous punishment in this world and the next, and they shall have none to help them." But as for those who believe and do what is right, he will pay them their reward, for God loves not the unjust. (Surah 33:47–50)

And peace upon me the day I was born, and the day I die, and the day I shall be raised up alive. (Surah 19:34)

And I was a witness against them so long as I was amongst them, but when thou didst cause me to die, thou wert the Watcher over them, for thou art witness over all. (Surah 5:117)

These texts certainly seem to teach that Jesus died. Yet in spite of them, Muslims everywhere quote the other verse when they deal with Christians, whom they accuse of misbelief:

And for their misbelief, and for their saying about Mary a mighty calumny, and for their saying, "Verily, we have killed the Messiah, Jesus the Son of Mary, the Apostle of God." . . . But they did not kill him and they did not crucify him, but a similitude was made for them. And verily, those who differ about him are in doubt concerning him; they have no knowledge concerning him, but only follow an opinion. They did not kill him, for sure! Nay, God raised him up into himself. (Surah 4:155–56)

In the traditions that have come down to us from the prophet himself (or that have been invented by his followers and attributed to Mohammed)[1] this denial of the death of Jesus Christ on the cross is elaborated. As apparently the death of Jesus Christ was both affirmed and denied in the Koran, to unify its teaching the only possible way of escape was to affirm that although he died for a few hours or days, he was not crucified. We read in the Muslim tradition:

And they spat upon him and put thorns upon him; and they erected the wood to crucify him upon it. And when they came to crucify him upon the tree, the earth was darkened, and God sent angels, and they descended between them and between Jesus; and God cast the likeness of Jesus upon him who had betrayed him, and whose name was Judas. And they crucified him in his [Jesus'] stead, and they thought that they crucified Jesus. Then God made Jesus to die for three hours, and then raised him up to heaven; and this is the meaning of the Koran verse: "Verily, I will cause thee to die, and raise thee unto me, and purify thee above those who misbelieve."[2]

In addition to this, Muslim commentators teach that when Christ comes again the second time, he will die, emphasizing, as it were, the frailty of his human nature, which even after his return from glory and his death for a few hours before his ascension, is still subject to death. This flatly contradicts all the teaching of the New Testament that "he died unto sin once" (Rom. 6:10) and "death hath no more dominion over him" (Rom. 6:9).

Not only do Muslims deny the historical fact of the crucifixion, but from the days of Mohammed himself until now, they have shown a strange and strong antipathy, and even a repugnance, to the very sign of the cross. It is related by al-Waqidi that Mohammed had such repugnance to the very form of the cross that he broke everything brought into his house with that figure upon it. This may have been mere superstition, or it may have been symbolical of his extreme aversion to the doctrine of the crucifixion.

According to Abu Hurairah, the prophet said, "I swear by heaven it is near when Jesus, the Son of Mary, will descend from heaven upon you people, a just king, and he will break the cross and kill the swine." In certain books of Muslim law it is expressly laid down under the head of theft that if a cross or crucifix is stolen from a church, the usual punishment for theft is not incurred, although if it be stolen from a private dwelling, it is a theft.

It is well known to readers of the daily press that Turkey and Egypt have never been willing to have Red Cross societies under the International Hague Convention regulations but have organized Red Crescent societies instead. A more recent incident illustrating Muslim hatred for the cross comes to us from the Sudan in connection with the postal service. The *United Empire* wrote:

> In the early days, the stamps of the Sudan bore a watermark which for many months passed unnoticed by their users. But one day a Muslim, in an idle moment, held one of them up to the light, and discovered to his dismay that this watermark bore an obvious resemblance to a Maltese cross. Now, to a devout Muslim, any suspicion of veneration to the cross of the Christian is not only distasteful; it is absolutely forbidden. And here for months the Muslim scribes of the Sudan had been placing their lips, or at least their tongues, to its hidden design unknowingly. . . . In the Sudan the authorities acted with discretion. They changed the watermark. Thus to philatelists a Sudan stamp watermarked with a design bearing a resemblance to a Maltese cross is a rather valuable discovery.

The Armenian massacres afforded other terrible instances of this fanatic hatred of the cross, the details of which can never be published. It is true, as Mr. Leeder states, that in the

Sahara and Tunisia the cross is used as a tattoo mark and in the decoration of weapons. This use of the cross, however, in certain parts of the Muslim world is due either to the fact that it has continued in use by tribes that were once Christian or that the symbol is of sinister import. The Tuaregs of the Sahara, as well as the Kabyles of North Africa, were undoubtedly once Christian.[3] And as regards the latter explanation, abundant proof exists in such works as those of El Buni on magic, talismans, and amulets. Near the Bab Al Fatooh in Cairo, Muslim women buy silver amulets specially made for them, consisting of a rude image of Christ on the cross, and on the back are verses from the Koran! It is well known that these are worn not to honor the Christ or the cross but with the intention of driving out demons by the use of a sign that is itself considered demonic!

Not only is the symbol of the cross a stumbling block to the Muslim mind, but also the doctrine of the cross is an offense. A number of books and pamphlets show this antipathy. Halil Halid in his book, *The Crescent versus the Cross*, shows how far even the educated Muslim carries this opposition. Halid is an honorary M.A. of Cambridge and a licentiate of the Institute of Law in Constantinople, and he writes:

> Islam also holds different views on the death of Christ. Whether historically correct or not, it does not admit the possibility of the crucifixion of Christ. It advances the theory that someone else must have been crucified by mistake in his place, as it cannot reconcile his lofty position with the alleged form of his death, a form which, to the Muslim mind, only befits criminals. To the Muslim mind it is not only sacrilegious, but also illogical at once to deify him and make him suffer such a death.

The Christian explanation that "Christ suffered that painful death for our sins" fails to satisfy the critics of the non-Christian world. It is doubtless convenient for many Christians to regard the passages of their Scriptures concerning the crucifixion as an insurance policy, and to conduct themselves in a manner which is hardly pious, feeling sure that they are safe against hellfire because Christ suffered for their sins. Mussulman critics say "what fanciful notions these Christians entertain on this subject! They not only state that the One, whom they are to worship, died such a death, but also make a mournful picture out of their notion of crucifixion, representing it by the fine arts—a picture which is neither realistic nor aesthetic."

Many of the most bitter attacks on Christianity by the Muslim press have been similarly directed against the cross and its teaching. In a book published at Beirut by Mohammed Tahir al Tannir, entitled *Pagan Elements in the Christian Religion,* the author draws a parallel between Krishna and Christ and even illustrates by crude wooden cuts Krishna's death and the death of Christ on the cross, the one with a crown of glory, the other with a crown of thorns! The book tries to prove that all Christian teaching regarding the crucifixion and the atonement is not based on historical fact but was borrowed piecemeal from heathenism.

Mohammed Tawfiq Sidqi, in a book entitled *Din Allah,* attacks the Christian faith both as regards its documents and its dogma, using the arguments of modern destructive criticism, without being aware that it is a two-edged sword which would play havoc with the Koran and the traditions if once its edge were tried. In the introduction he states that Christ is in no sense an atonement for sin and that ideas of sacrifice and

47

atonement are only remnants of heathenism. He attempts to prove that none of the prophecies of the Old Testament, especially not those found in Isaiah 53, Psalm 22, and Zechariah 12:13, refer in any way to Christ or to his death on the cross.

It is interesting to notice, however, how more and more the advocates of Islam and the opponents of Christianity among Muslims are becoming thoroughly aware that the doctrine of the cross is the Gibraltar of the Christian faith, the center and pivot of Christian theology, and the very foundation of the Christian hope. In an article published by Seyyid Mohammed Rashid Ridha in *Al Manar*, twelve pages are devoted to a rather candid inquiry regarding the crucifixion of Christ. In the very introduction of his subject the learned author says that "the belief in the crucifixion is the foundation of the Christian religion; if it were not for its doctrine of the cross and redemption, which are the root of the Christian religion, they would not spend time in calling upon men to accept and embrace it."

Following an exposition of the teaching of Christians, the article summarizes the objections to it as follows:

1. It is opposed to reason.
2. It is opposed to theism. How can God, who is omnipresent and everlasting, degrade himself by dwelling in a virgin's womb?
3. It is opposed to God's knowledge, for the plan of salvation—if such it is—was an afterthought.
4. It is opposed to both the mercy and justice of God; to his mercy because he allowed Christ to suffer, being innocent, without delivering him; and to his justice in allowing those who crucified him to do it unpunished.
5. It leads to impiety, because if this is the way of salvation, then no matter how wicked a man is, he finds de-

liverance through the cross and will never be punished for his sins.

6. It is unnecessary. We have never heard it stated by any reasonable person, or those who are learned in law, that the attribute of justice is abrogated by the pardon of a criminal. On the contrary, it is considered a virtue to pardon an offender. Why should not God do so?

From the above it is easy to judge that the modern standpoint of Islam is opposed not only to the historical fact of the crucifixion but also to the historical interpretation of that fact in Christian theology.

The question here arises: How can we account for Mohammed's repugnance to the crucifixion? Was it that he desired to defend the reputation of Jesus, the greatest prophet before him, from the stain that he considered was cast upon it by the Jews, who boasted that they had slain him (Surah 4:156)?

It may have been that to Mohammed's mind there was something abhorrent in the idea of a prophet being left to the mercy of his foes, especially in the case of one of the greater prophets. The Koran makes much of how God wrought deliverance for Noah, Abraham, Lot, and others, even by a miracle. It may have been that Mohammed, therefore, borrowing an idea of certain Christian sects, believed and taught that Christ was not crucified. The Basilidians, we are told, held that the person crucified was Simon of Cyrene. The Cyrenthians and Carpocratians believed that it was one of Jesus' followers, while the Persian heretic Mani taught that it was the prince of darkness himself.[4] Perhaps there was nothing to prevent Mohammed from adopting this view, as he was but imperfectly acquainted with the real doctrines of Christianity. We say, "perhaps," because another view is put forward by

Koelle in his philosophical study, on the historical position of Islam. He writes:

> Mohammed, from his low, earthly standing point, could neither apprehend the unique excellence of the character of Christ, nor the real nature of his all-sufficient and all-comprehending salvation.
>
> Not want of opportunity, but want of sympathy and compatibility, kept him aloof from the religion of Christ. His first wife introduced him to her Christian cousin; one of his later wives had embraced Christianity in Abyssinia, and the most favored of his concubines was a Christian damsel from the Copts of Egypt. He was acquainted with ascetic monks and had dealings with learned bishops of the Orthodox Church.[5]

Again, Mohammed was not ignorant of the supreme importance of the doctrine of the atonement. According to a well-known tradition, he said:

> I saw my Lord in the most beautiful form, and he said unto me, "O Mohammed, knowest thou on what subject the highest angels contend?" I answered, "Yes, O my Lord, on the subject of atonement, that is to say, on the services and degrees which are the cause of the atonement of sins." Thereupon the word was addressed to me, "What is atonement?" I answered, "Atonement is the remaining in the house of prayer after the service has been performed; the going to the meetings on foot; and the taking an ablution when trials and troubles befall: whoever does these things will live and die well, and be as pure from sin as if he had just been born of his mother."

Other traditions relate how Mohammed explained some of the pagan sacrifices, such as the 'Akika and the sacrifices at Mecca, as in a certain sense atoning for sin, so the doctrine of substitution could not, in itself, have been repugnant to him.[6]

Whatever the explanation may be, the fact remains that Islam from its origin until our own day has been an enemy of the cross of Christ and has ever made the crucifixion a cause of stumbling. This position, once taken by orthodox Islam, has been held throughout the centuries. The historical fact of Christ's crucifixion, with all it signifies to Christianity, has always been flatly contradicted.

Only among the Shiah sect in Persia do we have a remarkable illustration of the doctrine of the atonement and of substitution forcing a way for itself into Islam. The Aryan mind was never content with the barren monotheistic idea of the Semite Arabs. In Persia the doctrine of an incarnation, of intercessors, and of salvation by atonement found eager acceptance at an early date. Those who have witnessed the miracle play of Hassan and Hussein, commemorative of the events at Kerbela, will realize how large a place this death occupies in their life and thought as a propitiation for sin. At the close of the miracle play, the following words are put into the mouth of Mohammed:

> The key of paradise is in Hussein's hand. He is the mediator for all. Go thou and deliver from the flames everyone who has in his lifetime shed but a single tear for thee: everyone who has in any way helped thee; everyone who has performed a pilgrimage to thy shrine or mourned for thee. Bear each and all to paradise.[7]

In presenting this doctrine of the atonement, therefore, to Muslims of the Shiah sect, the story of Kerbela can be used to interpret that of Calvary and finds a response. At the Cairo missionary conference the Rev. S. G. Wilson, of Tabriz, gave this testimony: "When we are setting forth the story of the cross to Persians, they often reply, 'In like manner the blood of Imam Hussein avails for us as an offering to God.' This condition of belief prepares them to hear and understand the Christian doctrine of the atonement. It can be presented to them as to a Christian audience."

But how is it in regard to orthodox Islam? Should we emphasize this doctrine of the crucifixion where it is bitterly opposed and vigorously disputed? Would it not be the part of worldly wisdom and of missionary strategy to keep the cross and the atonement (as well as the doctrine of the Trinity) well in the background and present to Muslims the life of Christ rather than his death as the theme of our gospel? Shall we not follow the discretion (or was it the fear?) of the Sudan authorities in the matter of the postage stamps and remove even the watermark of the cross from our preaching lest we offend our Muslim brethren?

Let the apostle Paul give us the answer, that apostle who taught "that no man should put a stumbling block or an occasion to fall in his brother's way" (Rom. 14:13) and who made it a principle of his life that "if meat make my brother to offend, I will eat no flesh while this world standeth, lest I make my brother to offend" (1 Cor. 8:13). His reply would be in the words he wrote to the disputers of this world: "Christ crucified, unto the Jews a stumbling block, and unto the Greeks foolishness" (1 Cor. 1:23).

Paul knew that the cross was a stumbling block and the doctrine of the cross foolishness to Jew and Gentile, and yet he deliberately, emphatically, persistently, everywhere, made his mission and his message the cross. As we think of the millions in Muslim lands to whom our hearts go out in sympathy—their ignorance, their sinfulness, their utter need of the Savior—those other words of the apostle find new meaning: "For many walk, of whom I have told you often, and now tell you even weeping, that they are the enemies of the cross of Christ" (Phil. 3:18). Let us never on that account consider them our enemies but prove to them that we are their friends by showing not by our creed only, but by our lives, the power of the cross and its glory.

We must meet this earnest and latest challenge of our Muslim opponents not by compromises and concessions, nor by cowardice of silence, but by boldly proclaiming that the very heart of our religion, its center and its cynosure, its pivot and power, is the atonement wrought by Christ on the cross. We must show them that the cross is the highest expression of the very Spirit of Christ.

As Andrew Murray has said, the cross is his chief characteristic; that which distinguishes him from all in heaven and on earth; that which gives him his glory as Mediator on the throne through eternity. If faithfully, fearlessly, sympathetically, we preach Christ crucified, he can make the stumbling block of the cross a stepping stone for the Muslims into his kingdom.

There is no other way into that kingdom than the way of the cross. Only by the preaching of the cross can we expect among Muslims conviction of sin, true repentance, and faith in the merits of Another. The cross, and the cross alone, can break down their pride and self-righteousness and lay bare all hypocrisy and self-deception. More than this, the cross will win their love if rightly preached. The cross is the very antithesis of the spirit of Islam. It is the spirit of genuine Christianity. This issue must be made clear at the very outset, for it is wrapped up in every other truth of the Christian religion. Our conclusion, therefore, can find no better expression than in the words of Denny:

We may begin as wisely as we please with those who have a prejudice against it, or whose conscience is asleep, or who have much to learn both about Christ and about themselves before they will consent to look at such a gospel, to say nothing of abandoning themselves to it. But if we do not begin with something which is essentially related to the atonement, presupposing it or presupposed by it or involved in it, something which leads inevitably, though it may be by an indirect and unsuspected route, to the Lamb of God that taketh away the sin of the world, we have not begun to preach the gospel at all.[8]

CHAPTER
5

THE WAY TO THE
MUSLIM HEART

The only approach to the citadel of the will is through the mind or the heart. The way to convince a man against his will is to win that will by way of the intellect or the emotions to a new attitude and a new resolve. Dr. Fred F. Goodsell, for long years a missionary at Constantinople (Istanbul), points out this more excellent way. It is the language of love on human lips and in human lives. He writes from his experience:

> As we seek to confront Muslims with Jesus Christ, we must rely upon the dynamic fascination of radiant, Christlike living. This is the one single invincible thing about our Christian faith. It is more subtle than reasoned argument, more persuasive than an educational enterprise, and more effective than any amount

of formal religious instruction. Circumstances prevent one from telling of a number of cases where individuals have recently come to share Christ's life, not because of any word spoken to them about him but because he has been lived day in and day out in the community.

Fundamentally there are three reasons why hitherto so few Muslims have come to share our experience of Christ.

First, throughout their history they have been rigid and aggressive religionists, the most aggressive and militaristic of all religious people.

Second, from the very beginning the examples of Christ's way of life that they had before them were so repellent as to widen the breach rather than to bridge it. In a real sense it may be said that Islam is a Christian heresy that has based its appeal to religious minds on its protest against paganism in the Christian life and worship of its day.

Third, the Christian churches of the world have never seriously undertaken the task of evangelizing Muslim peoples.

Christ's way of life in Muslim lands has never won multitudes because it has never been lived among them on a noble scale over a considerable period of time. Christ's word stands: "And I, if I be lifted up, will draw all men unto me."

After forty years' experience—sometimes heartbreaking experience, of sowing on rocks and of watching the birds pick away the seed to the last grain—I am convinced that the nearest way to the Muslim heart is the way of God's love, the way of the cross.

Paul in his great chapter on this Christian love, as the true and excellent way, uses the Greek word *agape*. What that New Testament word connotes, in contrast with Plato's *eros*, is the subject of a monograph by the Swedish theologian Anders Nygren.[1] He comes to the conclusion that both in the New Testament and in the history of the church the idea of love is unique. Luther in his teaching brought out its full significance. Love in the Christian sense is primarily God's own love. "God is nothing but an abyss of eternal love." Christian love is spontaneous, overflowing. It is not like the world's love, evoked by the desire for its object. It is without respect of persons. It is love even for our enemies. "It is prepared freely to find its kindness thrown away and lost, as also Christ has found. For how could Christian love fare better in this world than the love of God and of Christ?"

It is this unique Pauline love, not a cold Platonic interest, that the missionary needs.

> Though I speak with the tongues of men and of angels, but have not love, I am become sounding brass or a clanging cymbal. Love suffereth long, and is kind; love envieth not; love vaunteth not itself, is not puffed up; doth not behave itself unseemly, seeketh not its own, is not provoked, taketh not account of evil; rejoiceth not in unrighteousness, but rejoiceth with the truth; beareth all things, believeth all things, hopeth all things, endureth all things. (1 Cor. 13:1, 4–7, author's paraphrase of KJV)

Where this is the attitude and character of the missionary, he will doubtless hear again from Muslim lips the words of the Koran: "And thou wilt find the nearest in love to those who believe to be those who say, We are Christians."

When we think of the spiritual unrest, the disappointed hopes, and disillusionments following the present chaos of political and social revolutions, we conclude that the hour is ripe for a ministry of love and reconciliation.

A passion for Muslim souls, however, does not mean that we are to compromise or to conciliate at any price. "Faithful are the wounds of a friend" (Prov. 27:6). There is a real sense in which he who loves Muslims most must often,

Like a skillful surgeon,
Go his way, and preach
On the old gospel's heart-assailing plan,
And cut the gangrene, like a practiced leech,
With firm, sure hand, and fear no face of man;
Call vile things vile; wash the fair paint from sin,
And give to glare of day the foul-faced sore within.

Yet this is only a small part of the cure of souls. The surgeon hurts to heal. The Great Physician is tender. In these days when Muslims are justly irritated by the political aggressions of Christian powers or the un-Christian conduct of the so-called representatives of Christianity, we may well emphasize the ministry of friendship and enter a plea for less of the spirit of controversy and more of the spirit of the cross.

Real Christians are the best and truest friends of Muslims everywhere and always. That is why travelers like Doughty met with kindness in the midst of fanaticism. It is only when travelers or politicians or missionaries do Christian things in an un-Christian way or when un-Christian things have been done by Christians that Christianity has appeared as a bitter foe to our Muslim friends. Not the Crusades but Raymund Lull represented real Christianity in the thirteenth century. Not the British bombardment of Jiddah in 1858 but the founding of Robert College in 1864 expressed the real desire of Christians toward the Near East.

In the Koran chapter "The Tablet" occurs a remarkable verse, the eighty-fifth, that expresses this same truth, only half comprehended by the prophet himself, and one that has never needed emphasis so much as it does today. "Thou wilt surely find the nearest in love to those who believe to be those who say, We are Christians; that is because there are among them priests and monks, and because they are not proud."

Baidhawi, the great Muslim writer, comments on this text as follows:

> Because of their gentleness and the tenderness of their hearts and their little desire for the present world, their much care for knowledge and labor; and to this the text has reference, that is because there are among them priests and monks and because they are not proud: i.e., to receive the truth when they understand it; or they are humble and not arrogant like the Jews. So this passage teaches that humility, a teachable spirit, and the fleeing from evil desires are praiseworthy even in the case of the infidel.

In spite of the sting at the end of this comment, Baidhawi and other commentators with him have here shown us the surest line of approach if we would win our Muslim brethren to Christ. Humility, docility, and love speak a language that is everywhere understood and that cannot be gainsaid. It was understood by Mohammed in the earlier part of his career when he met Christian monks and teachers, and it is understood today by his followers.

And this aspect of Christianity, and of our Savior himself, was well understood by the mystics in Islam. Again and again they call attention to the love of Jesus and the power of his spirit. Hallal-al-Din Al-Rumi wrote:

Thyself reckon dead, and then thou shalt fly
Free, free, from the prison of earth to the sky!
Spring may come, but on granite will grow no green
thing;
It was barren in winter, 'tis barren in spring;
And granite man's heart is, till grace intervene,
And, crushing it, clothe the long barren with green.
When the fresh breath of Jesus shall touch the
heart's core,
It will live, it will breathe, it will blossom once
more.[2]

If we remember, as we should, that Islam historically may be considered the prodigal son among the non-Christian religions, we will avoid the spirit of the elder brother and like the father in the matchless parable see him when he is yet a great way off, run out to meet him, and fall on his neck, and kiss him (Luke 15:20).

God loves the world of Islam, we may believe, because of their vast numbers. There are millions of little children in that multitude! He knows how long the church has neglected the task of evangelism. Our faithlessness has not changed this love. He knows better than anyone of those who try to win Muslims that they are "a great way off." Love is blind to faults and errors, but compassion has a hundred eyes, all open to human need. "They that are whole need not a physician; but they that are sick. I came not to call the righteous, but sinners to repentance" (Luke 5:31–32).

It was my privilege recently to worship with the brethren of the Moravian church in Bethlehem, Pennsylvania. Their missionary history is well known, but perhaps it is not so well known that in the litany used every Sunday morning there is a special prayer for the kingdom of God that includes the oldest missionary collect in the world. It goes back to Abraham, the father of the faithful and the friend of God, and sums up in one sentence his love for Ishmael, the prodigal son of the Old Testament. The litany reads as follows:

> O Lord, the hope of Israel, and the desire of all
>   nations:
> Have mercy on thy ancient covenant people, deliver
>   them from their blindness:
> O that Ishmael might live before thee.
> Prosper the endeavors of all thy servants to spread thy
>   gospel;
> Bless us and all other Christian congregations gath-
>   ered from among the heathen;
> Keep them as the apple of thine eye:
> Hear us, gracious Lord and God.
> O praise the Lord, all ye nations:
> Praise him, all ye people.

To hear a large congregation use this litany reminded me of the organization of our Arabian Mission in 1889. Professor J. G. Lansing chose this prayer of Abraham as the motto text for the new mission. It was his favorite text in preaching on missions to Muslims.

Face to face with the tragedy of Islam, the problem of its origin, the extent of its influence, the areas overshadowed by its darkness, saintly souls have again and again come back to that pathetic story of Ishmael, the exile. In a real sense, Islam is the prodigal son among the non-Christian religions. This faith arose six centuries after Christ and presents a problem essentially different from that of Hinduism and Buddhism and other ethnic faiths. When Mohammed, the prophet, turned his back on Jerusalem, toward which he first worshiped, and prayed toward Mecca, he went away to the far country of the prodigal.[3]

In a sense that Abraham never imagined, Ishmael has become a great nation. Arabia, next to Palestine, has become the mother of a spiritual world dominion.

Conscious of the destiny of this land and people on God's program for world redemption, Dr. J. G. Lansing in 1889 wrote the Arabian Mission hymn. This outburst of poetic love for Arabia has been the inspiration of the little band of pioneers for fifty years:

There's a land long since neglected,
There's a people still rejected,
But of truth and grace elected,
    In his love for them.

Softer than their night winds, fleeting,
Richer than their starry tenting,
Stronger than their sands protecting,
    Is his love for them.

To the host of Islam's leading,
To the slave in bondage bleeding,
To the desert dweller pleading,
    Bring his love to them.

Through the promise on God's pages,
Through his work in history's stages,
Through the cross that crowns the ages,
    Show his love to them.

With the prayer that still availeth,
With the power that prevaileth,
With the love that never faileth,
   Tell his love to them.

Till the desert's sons now aliens,
Till its tribes and their dominions,
Till Arabia's raptured millions,
   Praise his love of them.

That time is not yet, but the spirit of such love is the one great need in Muslim evangelism. Here is a brief passage from a letter written to me by an Armenian pastor at Aleppo. It breathes the same spirit of love:

During the Great War I was deported with my family from Adana to Aleppo. They were seeking out any Armenian to deport and separating men from women. They sought me by name. I hid myself in a dark and cold attic for six and a half months. In these terrible days my wife and I took our only son and dedicated him as a future worker among the Muslims. We thought that this was the shortest way of having our revenge from the fanatic and ferocious enemies. At present we are not allowed to show them what we think and feel, but we are expected to work in an attitude of prayer, and one day we shall find a good chance to show that we have kept warm the feeling of brotherhood towards them in spite of what they have been to us in the past.

If this spirit should take possession of the oriental churches, there would be a revival and an ingathering comparable to that of early Christianity when Saul of Tarsus witnessed the martyrdom of Stephen or when the disciples who were scattered by his persecution went everywhere preaching the word.

In one of his earliest epistles St. Paul defines the missionary activities of the Thessalonian church among their Gentile neighbors as "work of faith, and labor of love, and patience of hope" (1 Thess. 1:3). How accurately these three short phrases depict the real task of carrying the Good News to Muslims.

For thirteen long centuries, whether by neglect or by the pioneer adventure of loyal hearts, this part of the non-Christian world has tested the faith of Christendom as by fire. It has demanded a measure of love utterly impossible except to those who had learned from Christ to love their enemies and his; and again and again Islam has deferred the fruition of hope and left for those who waited on and on, as their only anchor, the patience of unanswered prayer.

Yet it is not the measure of our faith, the strength of our love, the steadfastness of our hope that are the determining factors in the evangelization of the world of Islam. The Author and Finisher of our faith and of all faith, the Source of all love, the patience of Christ incarnate waiting to see of the travail of his soul and be satisfied—all these challenge not us only but the Muslim world.

Wrote Bishop King:

We can many of us remember, in the days when we read *Ivanhoe*, the thrill which we felt when the doughty Saxon knight rode slowly on his warhorse up the lists and struck with sharpened lance the shield of Brian de Bois Guilbert "till it rang again." Such is the conception we formed of what is meant by a challenge. How different from this is the spiritual counterpart of which we speak! It is no steel-clad knight who comes before us, but Jesus in the tender majesty of his manhood. His crest is the cross of ignominy and pain; if he bears a spear, it is that which pierced his own side. The power which is his to set our hearts aflame for sacrifice is love tested to the uttermost by a sacrificial death. Christ himself is the Great Challenger. Shall we sit at ease, considering if we shall take the challenge or not?

PART 2

ISLAM AND ANIMISM

6

ANIMISM'S
INFLUENCE

That Islam in its origin and popular character is a composite faith, with pagan, Jewish, and Christian elements, is known to all students of comparative religion. Rabbi Geiger has shown how much of the warp and woof of the Koran was taken from Talmudic Judaism and how the entire ritual is simply that of the Pharisees translated into Arabic.[1] Tisdall in his "Sources of Islam" and other writers, especially Wellhausen, Goldziher, and Robertson Smith, have indicated the pagan elements that persist in the Muslim faith to this day and were taken over by Mohammed himself from the old Arabian idolatry. Christian teaching and life too had their influence on Mohammed and his doctrine, as is evident not only in the acknowledged place of honor given to Jesus Christ, the Virgin Mary, John the Baptist, and other New Testament characters, but also in the mystic beliefs and ascetic practices of later Islam.

"A threefold cord is not quickly [easily] broken" (Eccles. 4:3). The strength of Islam is its composite character. It entrenches itself everywhere and always in animistic and pagan superstition. It fights with all the fanatic devotion of Semitic Judaism with its exaggerated nationalism. It claims at once to include and supersede all that which Jesus Christ was and did and taught. It is a religion of compromise, of conservatism, and of conquest.

It is our purpose to show how strong is the pagan element in Islam. We will show how many doctrines and practices of popular Islam find their explanation only in a survival of the animism of ancient Arabia or were incorporated from many heathen sources in the spread of the faith, and how Islam was never able to eliminate or destroy these doctrines and practices. At the outset of our discussion it need not surprise us that a belief in demons and the old Arabian superstitions persisted in spite of Islam.

Five times daily the Muslim muezzin calls out from the mosque: "There is no god but Allah." The people repeat this and reiterate it far more than a hundred times during the day in their quarrels, feasts, fasts, rejoicings, and common conversation. But in my daily observations—and I have lived among them for more than twenty-five years—I find they have fetishes and superstitious customs that amount to as many gods as the heathen who bow down to wood and stone.

Now we find that Islam in Arabia itself and in the older Muslim lands was not able to shake itself free from similar beliefs and practices. To understand these fully in their origin and character it is necessary first of all to know something of what we mean by animism. Animism is the belief that a great part, if not all of the inanimate kingdom of nature, as well as all animated beings, are endowed with reason, intelligence, and volition identical with man. Kennedy defines it as "both a religion, a system of philosophy and a system of medicine. As a religious system it denotes the worship of spirits as distinguished for that of the gods."[2] Warneck states that

> it would seem as if Animism were the primitive form of heathenism, maintaining itself, as in China and India to this hour, amid all the refinements of civilization. The study of Greek and old German religions exhibits the same animistic features. The essence of heathenism seems to be not the denial of God, but complete estrangement from Him. The existence of God is everywhere known, and a certain veneration given him. But He is far away, and is therefore all but ruled out of the religious life. His place is taken by demons, who are feared and worshiped.[3]

Even in Arabia the stern monotheism of the Wahabi reformers was unable to eradicate the pagan superstitions of Islam because they are imbedded in the Koran and were not altogether rejected by Mohammed himself, and much less by his companions.

With regard to the pagan practices prevalent in early Islam, Abu'l Fida calls attention to a number of religious observances that were thus perpetuated under the new system.

> The Arabs of the times of ignorance used to do things which the religious law of Islam has adopted. They used to not wed their mothers or their daughters, and among them it was deemed a most detestable thing to marry two sisters. They used to revile the man who married his father's wife, and to call him *Daizan*.
>
> They, moreover, used to make the pilgrimage (Hajj) to the House [the Kaaba], and to visit the con-

secrated places, and wear the Ihram [the single garment worn to the present day by a pilgrim when run-
ning round the Kaaba], and perform the Tawwaf, and
run [between the hills As Safā and Al Marwa], and
make their stand at all the Stations and cast the stones
[at the devil in the valley of Mina], and they were
wont to intercalate a month every third year.

He goes on to mention many other similar examples in which
the religion of Islam has enjoined as religious observances ancient Arabian customs, for instance, ceremonial washings after certain kinds of defilement, parting the hair, the ritual
observed in cleansing the teeth, paring the nails, and other
such matters.[4]

Mohammed also borrowed certain fables current among the
heathen Arabs, such as the tales of Ad and Thamud and some
others (Surah 7:63–77). Regarding such stories, Al Kindi well
says to his opponent: "And if thou mentionest the tale of Ad and
Thamud and the Camel and the Comrades of the Elephant"
(Surahs 105 and 14:9) "and the like of these tales, we say to thee,
'These are senseless stories and the nonsensical fables of old
women of the Arabs, who kept reciting them night and day.'"

When we read the account of pre-Islamic worship at
Mecca, we realize how many of the ancient customs persist in
Islam. The principal idols of Arabia were the following:

- *Hobal* was in the form of a man and came from Syria.
  He was the god of rain and had a high place of honor.
- *Wadd* was the god of the firmament. Special prayers
  for rain and against eclipse were taught by Mohammed.
- *Suwah* was in the form of a woman. She was said to be
  from antediluvian times.

- *Yaghuth* had the shape of a lion.
- *Ya'ook* was in the form of a horse. He was worshiped in Yemen. (Bronze images of this idol are found in ancient tombs and are still used as amulets.)
- *Nasr* was the eagle god.
- *El Uzza*, identified by some scholars with Venus, was worshiped at time under the form of an acacia tree.
- *Allat* was the chief idol of the tribe of Thakif at Taif, who tried to compromise with Mohammed to accept Islam if he would not destroy their god for three years. The name appears to be the feminine of Allah.
- *Manat* was a huge stone worshiped as an altar by several tribes.
- *Duwar* was the virgin's idol. Young women used to go around it in procession, hence its name.
- *Isaf* and *Naila* were idols that stood near Mecca on the hills of Safa and Mirwa. The visitation of these popular shrines is now a part of the Muslim pilgrimage (i.e., they perpetuate ancient idolatrous rites).
- *Habhab* was a large stone on which camels were slaughtered. In every Muslim land sacred stones, sacred trees, and so on, abound. In most cases these were formerly shrines of pagan, and in some cases Christian, sanctity.

"Even in the higher religions," says Warneck, "and in the heathenism that exists in Christendom, we find numerous usages of animistic origin. Buddhism, Confucianism, and Islam have nowhere conquered this most tenacious of all forms of religion. They have not even entered into conflict with it. It is only overcome by faith in Jesus Christ." Therefore these many superstitions can now no longer be styled anti-Islam, although they conflict in many respects with the original doctrines of Islam. A religion is not born full-grown any more than a man. If on attaining a ripe maturity it has cast off the form of its early youth past recognition, we cannot deny it its right to this transformation, as it is part and parcel of the scheme of nature.

Writes Dr. Snouck Hurgronje:

A custom or idea does not necessarily stand condemned according to the Muslim standard, even though in our minds there can be no shadow of doubt as to its pagan origin. If, for example, Muslim teaching is able to regard some popular custom as a permissible enchantment against the devil or against jinns hostile to mankind, or as an invocation of the mediation of a prophet or saint with God, then it matters not that the existence of these malignant spirits is actually only known from pagan sources, nor does any one pause to inquire whether the saint in question is but a heathen god in a new dress, or an imaginary being whose name but serves to legitimate the existing worship of some object of popular reverence.[5]

Some writers go so far as to say that animism lies at the root of all Muslim thinking and all Muslim theology. "The Muslim," says Gottfried Simon, "is naturally inclined to animism; his animism does not run counter to the ideal of his religion. Islam is the classic example of the way in which the non-Christian religions do not succeed in conquering animism." He continues:

This weakness in face of the supreme enemy of all religious and moral progress bears a bitter penalty. Among the animistic peoples Islam is more and more entangled in the meshes of animism. The conqueror is, in reality, the conquered.

Islam sees the most precious article of its creed, the belief in God, and the most important of its religious acts, the profession of belief, dragged in the mire of animistic thought. Only in animistic guise do they gain currency among the common people. Instead of Islam raising the people, it is itself degraded. Islam, far from delivering heathendom from the toils of animism, is itself deeply involved in them. Animism emerges from its struggle for the soul of a people, modernized it is true, but more powerful than ever, elegantly tricked out and buttressed by theology. Often it is scarcely recognizable in its refined Arabian dress, but it continues as before to sway the people; it has received divine sanction.

Other writers express a still stronger opinion. "Muslim ritual, instead of bringing a man to God," writes Dr. Adriani, "serves as a drag net for Animism," and evidence confirms this from Celebes, where the Muslim is more superstitious even than the heathen. "Islam has exercised quite different influence upon the heathen from what we should expect. It has not left him as he was, nor has it tempered his Animism. Rather it has relaid the old animistic foundations of the heathen's religion and run up a light, artistic superstructure upon it of Muslim customs."[6]

While Muslims profess to believe in one God and repeat his glorious incommunicable attributes in their daily worship, they everywhere permit this glorious doctrine to be buried under a mass of pagan superstitions borrowed either originally from the demon worship of the Arabs, the Hindu gods, or the animistic practices of Malaysia and Central Africa. Regarding the millions of Muslims of Indonesia Wilkinson well says:

The average Malay may be said to look upon God as upon a great king or governor, mighty, of course, and just, but too remote a power to trouble himself about a villager's petty affairs; whereas the spirits of the district are comparable to the local police, who may be corrupt and prone to error, but who take a most absorbing personal interest in their radius of influence, and whose ill-will has to be avoided at all costs.

At first consideration one would imagine that the stern monotheism of Islam—the very intolerance of Semitic belief in Allah—would prevent compromise with polytheism. The facts are, however, to the contrary. "Belief in spirits of all sorts is neither peculiar to Acheh nor in conflict with the teaching of Islam," says Hurgronje.

Actual worship of these beings in the form of prayer might seriously imperil monotheism, but such worship is a rare exception in Acheh. The spirits most believed in are hostile to mankind and are combated by exorcism. The manner in which this is done in Acheh, as in Arabia and other Muslim countries is at variance in many respects with the orthodox teaching. Where, however, the Achenese calls in the help of these spirits of other methods of enchantment in order to cause ill-fortune to his fellow man, he does so with the full knowledge that he is committing a sin.

The missionary Gottfried Simon goes even further when he says:

The pioneer preaching of the Muslim idea of God finds a hearing all the more easily because it does not essentially rise above the level of animistic ideas. The Muslim does not bring the heathen something absolutely new with his doctrine of God; his idea of God correlates itself to existing conceptions. Animism is really the cult of spirits and the souls of the departed. Yet spirit worship has not been able to entirely obliterate the idea of God.[7]

He goes on to show that among all the tribes of Sumatra, the images that are incorrectly called idols are either pictures to scare away evil spirits by their ugliness, or soul carriers, that is to say, pictures into which soul stuff has been introduced by some kind of manipulation. They therefore either introduce soul stuff into the house (soul stuff = life power, life fluid, hence a material conception) and with it a blessing, or by an increase of soul stuff they ensure protection against diseases and spirits. The first group might perhaps best be called amulets, or when they are worshiped and given food, fetishes; and the second group, talismans.

In Skeat's *Malay Magic* it is shown that just as in the language of the Malays one can pick out Arabic words from the main body of native vocabulary, so in their popular religious customs Muslim ideas overlie a mass of original pagan notions.

The Malays of the Peninsula are Sunni Muslims of the school of Shafi'i, and nothing, theoretically speaking, could be more correct and orthodox (from the point of view of Islam) than the belief which they profess. But the beliefs which they actually hold are another matter altogether, and it must be admitted that the Muslim veneer which covers their ancient superstitions is very often of the thinnest description.

The inconsistency in which this involves them is not, however, as a rule realized by themselves. Beginning their invocations with the orthodox preface, "In the name of God, the merciful, the compassionate," and ending them with an appeal to the creed, "There is no god but God, and Muhammad is the Apostle of God," they are conscious of no impropriety in addressing the intervening matter to a string of Hindu divinities, demons, ghosts, and nature spirits, with a few angels and prophets thrown in, as the occasion may seem to require.[8]

The Wider Extent of Animism

The very wide extent of animism is often not realized. This belief is the living, working creed of over half the human race. All South, Central, and West African tribes are animists, except where animism has been dispossessed by Christianity. The Islam of Africa is largely mingled with it. It is the faith of Madagascar. North and South American Indians knew no other creed when Columbus landed, and the uncivilized remnant still profess it. The islanders of the Pacific and the aborigines of Australia are animists. In Borneo and the Malay Archipelago it is strong, although a good deal affected by Hinduism. Even in China and Japan, its adherents are numbered by the millions. In Burma it has been stated that the nominal Buddhism of the country is in reality only a thin veneer over the real religion, which is animism. In India, while the census reports record only a relatively low number of animists, yet there are probably more than ten times that number whose Hinduism displays little else, and even the Muslims in many places are affected by it.

There is no agreement among scholars regarding the origin of animism. According to a writer in the *Encyclopedia Britannica*, "Animism may have arisen out of or simultaneously with animatism as a primitive explanation of many different phenomena. If animatism was originally applied to non-human or inanimate objects, animism may from the outset have been in vogue as a theory of the nature of men."

"Lists of phenomena from the contemplation of which the savage was led to believe in Animism have been given," the writer continues. "Among these phenomena are trance and unconsciousness, sickness, death, clairvoyance, dreams, apparitions of the dead, wraiths, hallucinations, echoes, shadows and reflections. According to this theory evolution accounts for the growth of religious ideas. But all are not in accord with this theory. It is opposed to the Scriptures."

Says Warneck:

A dispassionate study of heathen religions confirms the view of Paul that heathenism is a fall from a better knowledge of God. In earlier days humanity had a greater treasure of spiritual goods. But the knowledge of God's eternal power and divinity was neglected. The Almighty was no longer feared or worshiped and dependence upon Him was renounced. This downward course was continued till nothing but a dim presentiment of Him was left. The creature stepped into the place of the Creator, and the vital power, the soul-stuff and the spirits of the dead came to be worshiped.[9]

This view is not exploded by science, for the *Encyclopedia Britannica* concludes its discussion on the subject by saying, "Even, therefore, if we can say that at the present day the gods are entirely spiritual, it is clearly possible to maintain that they have been spiritualized *pari passu* with the increasing importance of the animistic view of nature and of the greater prominence of eschatological beliefs. The animistic origin of religion is therefore not proven."

Aside from the question of origin, we return to its content. It is in its reaching regarding man's soul and the supreme importance of the immaterial that animism affords a point of contact with such words of Christ as "what shall it profit a man, if he shall gain the whole world, and lose his own soul?" (Mark 8:36). It is the loss of the soul, the spirit, the invisible life principle that the animist fears. This fear brings him into a lifelong bondage to superstitions.

Among the Basutos in Africa it is held that a man walking by the brink of a river may lose his life if his shadow falls on the water, for a crocodile may seize it and draw him in. In Tasmania and in North and South America, the conception is found that the soul is somehow identical with the shadow of a man. For some of the American Indians the Roman custom of receiving the breath of a dying man was no mere pious duty but a means of ensuring that his soul was transferred to a new body.

Other familiar conceptions identify the soul with the liver or the heart, with the reflected figure seen in the pupil of the eye, and with the blood. Although the soul is often distinguished from the vital principle, there are many cases in which a state of unconsciousness is explained as due to the absence of the soul. In South Australia *wilyamarraba* (without soul) is the word used for "insensible." So too the autohypnotic trance of the magician or shaman is regarded as due to his visit to distant regions or the nether world, of which he brings back an account.

In many parts of the world it is held that the human body is the seat of more than one soul. In the island of

Nias four are distinguished, the shadow and the intelligence, which die with the body, a tutelary spirit, termed *begoe*, and a second which is carried on the head. . . .

Just as among western nations the ghost of a dead person is held to haunt the church-yard or the place of death, although more orthodox ideas may be held by the same person as to the nature of a future life, he, more consistently, assigns different abodes to the multiple souls with which he credits man.

Of the four souls of a Dakota Indian one is held to stay with the corpse, another in the village, a third goes into the air, while the fourth goes to the land of souls, where its lot may depend on its rank in this life, its sex, mode of death or sepulture, on the due observance of funeral ritual, or many other points. From the belief in the survival of the dead arose the practice of offering food and lighting fires at the grave, at first as an act of friendship or filial piety, later as an act of worship.

The simple offering of food or shedding of blood at the grave develops into an elaborate system of sacrifice. Even where ancestor worship is not found, the desire to provide the dead with comforts in the future life may lead to the sacrifice of wives, slaves or animals, to the breaking or burning of objects at the grave or to the corpse to pay the traveling expenses of the soul. But all is not finished with the passage of the soul to the land of the dead. The soul may return to avenge its death by helping to discover the murderer, or to wreak vengeance for itself. There is a widespread belief that those who die a violent death become malignant spirits and endanger the lives of those who come near the haunted spot. The woman who dies in child-birth becomes a *pontianak,* and threatens the life of human beings. Man resorts to magical or religious means of repelling his spiritual dangers.[10]

It is clear from the beliefs of the non-Muslims of Malaysia that all things, organic and inorganic, were once credited with the possession of souls. This primitive animism survives most distinctly in the well-known Muslim Malay ceremonies connected with the rice soul at seedtime or harvest, but it is also traceable in a large number of other practices. We are told that whenever a peasant injures anything he must propitiate its personality, its living essence, its soul, its tutelary spirit—call it what we will. If the hunter slays a deer, he must excuse himself. It is not the man but the gun or the knife or the leaden bullet that must answer for the deed. Should a man wish to mine or to set up a house, he must begin by propitiating the spirits of the turned-up soil. Should he desire to fish, he will address the spirits of the sea and even the fish themselves. Should he contemplate planting, he begins by acknowledging that rice has a living essence of its own that he is bound to treat with respect. In short, he considers that all nature is teeming with life and that his own soul is walking in the midst of invisible foes.

All of these evil spirits find worshipers among Muslims in the Malay States today. The *pawang* or witch doctor and not the Muslim priest is called in to exorcise them. This he does with old-fashioned magic with admixture of the names of Allah and Mohammed. "The *pawang* or witch-doctor is in great demand by orthodox Muslim Malays, especially in times of sickness, although he often appeals openly to Siva or uses such language as the following:

"I am the equal of the Archangels,
I sit upon God's Judgement-seat,
And lean on the pillar of God's Throne of Glory."[11]

In reading a standard work on Animism by Kruijt I noted the following particulars in which animism and Islam agree. The correspondence is the more remarkable because my experiences have been limited to East Arabia and Egypt. That is to say, Islam in its cradle already had these features of paganism or primitive animism:

The putting of blood upon the doorposts and the foundations when a house is being built. The special importance of the placenta as a double of the child. Hair as the seat of the soul. Among the pagans there are ceremonies connected with the shaving of the hair in infancy. The Toradjas nail bits of the human scalp or shreds of hair to the palm trees to make them more fruitful. The same is done with the hair of infants. When a mother leaves her child for a journey, she ties some of her own hair to that of the child so that "the child believes the mother is still present." Hair offerings take place as in Islam.

The fingernails are connected with the soul and have spiritual value. Also the teeth. Spittle, perspiration, tears, and the other excretions of the body all contain soul stuff, and one may see in all the superstitions of the animist the same practices that are related of Mohammed the prophet and his companions in Muslim tradition.

The use of urine as medicine is not more common among pagans of Celebes than in Muslim lands where the practice of Mohammed the prophet and his teaching is still supreme. One needs only to consult books like Ed Damiri or Tub-en-Nabawi. The use of blood of animals, of saliva, of blowing, spitting, and stroking in order to bring benefit to the patient is universal among animists. This was also common in early Islam and is today. It is recorded in early tradition that Mohammed practiced cures in this manner. In Java and Sumatra spitting is a common method for curing the sick. Among animists amulets and anklets are worn to keep the soul in the body. At the time of death the nose, the ears, and the mouth are carefully plugged up to prevent the soul from escaping. These customs at the time of burial are universal also in Islam.

Among animists, sneezing is considered unfortunate, for then the soul tries to escape from the body. Yawning is on the other hand a good sign, for the breath comes inward. Perhaps for this reason the Muslims everywhere ask forgiveness of God when they sneeze but praise him when they yawn.

The belief that souls of men may inhabit animals such as dogs, cats, gazelles, and snakes is animistic. The same is taught in Muslim books, for example in "The Arabian Nights," which gives us a faithful picture of popular Islam. The bones of animals contain soul matter and are therefore dreaded by the animist or used for special purposes of good or ill. We may connect with this the belief of the Muslims that bones are the food of jinn and must not be touched. Mr. Kruijt shows in chapter 6 of his book that soul stuff exists in certain metals, iron, gold, silver, and lead. These are therefore powerful protectors against evil spirits. Iron objects are used to defend infants in the cradle. The same practice is carried on in Arabia, Egypt, Persia, and Morocco.

The soul after death takes its flight into the animal kingdom. Souls change especially to dwell in butterflies, birds, mice, lizards, and snakes. May we not connect with this the teaching of Islam that the souls of Muslim martyrs go into the crops of green birds until the resurrection day? Or closer yet is the common belief in metempsychosis based upon Koran legends, developed in the commentaries. Does not the Koran teach that Jews were changed into apes and tradition tell us that Jews and Christians were changed into hogs?

When we read the pages of Kruijt on the fetish, we are struck in almost every paragraph with parallel beliefs current in Islam. Stones are sacred because they contain spirits. Trees are sacred for the same reason:

> If a man has been successful in fighting, it has not been his natural strength of arm, quickness of eye, or readiness of resource that has won success. He has certainly got the mana of a spirit or of some deceased warrior to empower him, conveyed in an amulet of a stone round his neck, or a tuft of leaves in his belt, in a tooth hung upon a finger of his bow hand, or in the form of words with which he brings supernatural assistance to his side.

Word for word this might be said of Muslims today.

With regard to stone worship Kruijt tells us of sacred stones in the Indian Archipelago that receive worship because they fell from heaven (cf. the Black Stone at Mecca) or because of their special shape. Among the Dajaks of Serawak, Chalmers tells of the interior of a Lundu house at one end of which were collected the relics of the tribe. "These consisted of several round-looking stones, two deer heads, and other inferior trumpery. The stones turn black if the tribe is to be beaten in war and red if to be victorious. Anyone touching them would be sure to die and if they were lost, the tribe would be ruined." The Black Stone at Mecca is also believed to have changed color. Tree worship, by hanging amulets on the tree to produce fertility or bring blessing, is common in Celebes and New Guinea not only, but in Arabia, Egypt, and Morocco.

The effect of all this, even on the conception of God in Islam, is of importance. Here also there are points of contact as well as points of contrast. Warneck asks:

> What has animism made of God, the holy and gracious Creator and Governor of the world? It has divested him of his omnipotence, his love, his holiness and righteousness and has put him out of all relation with man. The idea of God has become a mere decoration; his worship a caricature. Spirits inferior to men, whose very well-being is dependent on men's moods, are feared instead of the Almighty. The rule of an inexorable fate is substituted for the wise and good government of God. Absurd lies are believed concerning the life after death, and efforts are made to master the malevolent spirits by a childish magic.

Is this not true of Arabia also?

Regarding the impotence of Islam to reject animistic influences that have dragged down to its lowest levels the ideas of God, Warneck goes on to say:

> Islam, even with its higher idea of God, cannot introduce into the heathenism which it influences any development for the better. The heathen, who have passed over to Islam, quietly retain their demon worship. Instead of the purer idea of God raising them, they drag it down to their own level, a proof of the tremendous down-drag which animistic religions possess.

"Islam," he says in another place, "has been unable to remove the fear of evil spirits. On the contrary, it assists in the expulsion of the spirits by its *malims*. It allows the people to go on worshiping ancestors and adds new spirits of Arabic origin to those already worshiped. Islam nowhere appears among animists as a deliverer."

The missionary is not so much concerned after all with the fact of animism in Islam as he is with the failure of Islam to meet animistic practices and overcome them. Gottfried Simon has shown conclusively that Islam cannot uproot pagan practices or remove the terror of spirits and demon worship in Sumatra and Java.[12] This is true everywhere. In its conflict with animism Islam has not been the victor.[13]

Points of Contact and Contrast

Animism in Islam offers points of contact and contrast that may well be used by the missionary. Christianity's message and power must be applied to the superstitions of Islam and especially to pagan practices. The fear of spirits can be met by the love of the Holy Spirit and the terror of death by the repose and confidence of the Christian. True exorcism is not found in the *zar* but in prayer. So-called demonic possession can often be cured by medical skill and superstition rooted out by education. Jesus Christ is the Lord of the unseen world, especially the world of demons and angels. Christ points out the true ladder of Jacob and the angels of God ascending and descending upon the Son of man. He is the sole channel of communication with the other world. With him as our living, loving Savior and Friend we have no fear of "the arrow that flieth by day; nor for the pestilence that walketh in darkness" (Ps. 91:5–6).

A Guide for Students

In order to guide students for further study in regard to animism and Islam we give certain keys that will unlock the subject; for if Muslims know that we have some idea of their superstition they will tell us more. The subject needs thorough investigation, especially in Egypt.

The best book on animism is by the late A. C. Kruijt, a Dutch missionary in the East Indies (Indonesia), and his division of the subject is very suggestive. I here translate the table of contents of his book. Every subject leads out into a wide field of thought and investigation.

I. ANIMISM

1. The personal soul stuff of man found especially in the head, the intestines, the blood, placenta, hair, teeth, saliva, sweat, tears, urine, etc.
2. Means by which this soul stuff is appropriated, e.g., spitting, blowing, blood wiping, and touch.
3. The personal soul in man: the shadow, the dream, the escape of the soul through sneezing, yawning, etc. The werewolf and the witch.
4. The soul stuff of animals.
5. Soul stuff of plants, sacred plants.
6. Soul stuff of inanimate objects—metals, iron, gold, etc.
7. The transmigration of the soul, especially in animals—the firefly, the butterfly, the birds, the mouse, the snake, the lizard.
8. Special honor paid to animals, fetishes, stones, and amulets.

II. SPIRITISM, OR THE DOCTRINE OF THE SOUL

1. The living man—in regard to his soul, its nature.
2. The life of the soul after death—it remains in the grave or in the house—its journey to soul land.

3. The worship of souls—either through a medium or without a medium—in special places or in special objects. The priesthood that gives communication with the souls of the departed.

III. DEMONOLOGY

1. Introduction of the creator and creation.
2. The spiritual part of creation.
3. Animals as messengers of the gods.
4. Predestination.
5. Honor of man—saint worship.
6. Demigods.
7. The home of the gods.
8. Agricultural gods and sea gods.
9. Tree spirits and other demons.
10. How demons show themselves and how one drives them away.

CHAPTER
7

THE FAMILIAR SPIRIT OR QARINA

Among all the superstitions in Islam there is none more curious in its origin and character than the belief in the *qarin* or *qarina*. It probably goes back to the ancient religion of Egypt or to the animistic beliefs common in Arabia as well as in Egypt at the time of Mohammed. By *qarin* or *qarina* the Muslim understands the double of the individual, his companion, his mate, his familiar demon: in the case of males a female mate, and in the case of females a male. This double is generally understood to be a devil, *shaitan*, or jinn, born at the time of the individual's birth and his constant companion throughout life. The *qarina* is, therefore, of the progeny of Satan.

There are many passages in the Koran in which this doctrine is plainly taught, and by reading the commentaries on these texts, a world of superstition, groveling, coarse, and, to the last degree, incredible, is opened to the reader. The Koran reads as follows: "And when we said to the angels, 'Adore Adam,' they adored him, save only Iblis, who was of the jinn, who revolted from the bidding of his Lord. 'What! will ye then take him and his seed as patrons, rather than me, when they are foes of yours? Bad for the wrong-doers is the exchange!'" The reference here is to the words "Satan and his seed" (Chapter of the Cave, verse 48).[1]

In speaking of the resurrection when the trumpet is blown and the day of judgment comes, the Koran reads:

> And every soul shall come — with it a driver and a witness! "Thou wert heedless of this, and we withdrew thy veil from thee, and today is thine eyesight keen!" And his mate (*qarina*) shall say, "This is what is ready for me [to attest]." "Throw into hell every stubborn misbeliever! He forbids good, a transgressor, a doubter! He sets other gods with God. Throw him, ye twain, into fierce torment!" His mate shall say, "Our Lord! I seduced him not, but he was in a remote error." He shall say, "Wrangle not before me; for I sent the threat to you before. The sentence is not changed with me, nor am I unjust to my servants." On the day we will say to hell, "Art thou full?" and it will say, "Are there any more?" (Chapter Kaf, verses 22–31)

And again the Koran says:

> And those who expend their wealth in alms for appearance sake before men, and who believe not in God nor in the last day; But whosoever has Satan for his mate, an evil mate has he (Chapter of Women, verses 41–42).

Again:

... and with them damsels, restraining their looks, large eyed, as though they were a sheltered egg. And some shall come forward to ask others, and a speaker amongst them shall say: "Verily, I had a mate (*qarina*), who used to say, 'Art thou verily of those who credit? What! when we are dead, and have become earth and bones, shall we be surely judged?' " He will say, "Are ye looking down?" And he shall look down and see him in the midst of hell. He shall say, "By God, thou didst nearly ruin me!" (Chapter of the Ranged, verses 47–54)

We will allot to them mates, for they have made seemly to them what was before them and what was behind them. And due against them was the sentence on the nations who passed away before them, both of jinns and of mankind. Verily, they were the losers! (Chapter Detailed, verse 24).

And whosoever turns from the remainder of the Merciful One, we will chain to him a devil, who shall be his mate; and, verily, these shall turn them from the path while they reckon that they are guided; until when he comes to us he shall say, "O, would that between me and thee there were the distance of the two orients, for an evil mate [art thou]!" But it shall not avail you on that day, since ye were unjust; verily, in the torment shall ye share! (Chapter of Gilding, verses 35–37).

These passages leave no doubt that the *qarina*, which has been the mate of the believer all through life, is cast into hell on the day of judgment, and that this evil spirit, which is born with every man, is determined to ruin him. But the favor of God saves the believer, and one of the special mercies of heaven for the believer is to behold his companion devil forever in torment.

Before we deal further with the comment as given on these verses and the teaching in Muslim books, we may well consider the possible origin of this belief as found in the "Book of the Dead" of ancient Egypt. Writes E. A. Wallis Budge:

> In addition to the Natural-body and Spirit-body, man also had an abstract individuality or personality endowed with all his characteristic attributes. This abstract personality had an absolutely independent existence. It could move freely from place to place, separating itself from, or uniting itself to, the body at will, and also enjoying life with the gods in heaven. This was the *ka*, a word which at times conveys the meaning of its Coptic equivalent *kw*, and of *eidolon*, image, genius, double, character, disposition, and mental attributes. What the *ka* really was has not yet been decided, and Egyptologists have not yet come to an agreement in their views on the subject.[2]

Whatever may be the significance of *ka* in Egyptology, we are not in doubt as to what Mohammed himself thought of his *ka* or *qarina*. In the most famous volume of all Muslim books on the doctrine of jinn, called "Kitab akam ul marjan fi Ahkam el Jan," by Abdullahesh-Shabli, we read in chapter 5 as follows:

> It is related about 'Ayesha that the Apostle of God, Mohammed, left her one night and that she said, "I

was jealous of him." Then she said, "Mohammed saw me and came for me and said, 'What's the matter with you, 'Ayesha? Are you jealous?'" And I replied, "Why should one like me not be jealous of one like you?" Then the Apostle of God said, "Has your devil spirit got hold of you?" Then I said, "O Apostle of God, is there a devil with me?" Said he, "Yes, and with every person." Said I, "And with you also, O Apostle of God?" Said he, "Yes but my Lord Most Glorious and Powerful has assisted me against him, so that he became a Muslim."

Another tradition is given in the same chapter on the authority of Ibn Hanbal as follows: "Said the apostle of God, 'There is not a single one of you but has his *qarina* of the jinn and his *qarina* of the angels.' They said, 'And thou also, O Apostle of God?' 'Yes,' he replied, 'I also, but God has helped her so that she does not command me except in that which is true and good.'" The tradition given here occurs in many forms in the same chapter, so that there can be no doubt of its being well known and, in the Muslim sense, authentic.

Here is another curious form of the same tradition. "Said the Apostle of God, 'I was superior to Adam in two particulars, for my devil (*qarina*), although an unbeliever, became through God's help a Muslim. And my wives were a help to me, but Adam's devil remained an infidel and his wife led him into temptation.'" We also find an evening prayer recorded of Mohammed as follows: "Whenever the Apostle of God went to his bed to sleep at night he said, 'In the name of God I now lay myself down and seek protection from him against the evil influence of my devil (*qarin*, *shaitan*), and from the burden of my sin and the weight of my iniquity. O God, make me to receive the highest decree.'"

As regards the number of these companion devils and their origin, tradition is not silent.

It is said that there are males and females among the devils, out of whom they procreate; but as to Iblis, God has created . . . [the significance of this passage, which is not fit for translation, is that Iblis is a hermaphrodite, possessing the organs of both sexes] . . . there come forth out of him every day ten eggs, out of each of which are born seventy male and female devils.[3]

In another tradition also found in the standard collections it is said that Iblis laid thirty eggs—

ten in the west, ten in the east, and ten in the middle of the earth—and that out of every one of those eggs came forth a species of devils, such as al-Gilan, al-'Akarib, al-Katarib, al-Jann, and others bearing diverse names. They are all enemies of men according to the words of God, "What! will ye then take him and his seed as patrons, rather than we, when they are foes of yours?" with the exception of the believing ones among them.

Et-Tabari, in his great commentary (26:104) says the *qarin* or *qarina* is each man's *shaitan* (devil), who was appointed to have charge of him in the world. He then proves his statement by a series of traditions similar to those already quoted: "His *qarin* is his devil (*shaitan*)"; "His *qarina* is his jinn."

According to Muslim tradition, not only Mohammed but even Jesus the Prophet had a *qarin*. As Jesus was sinless, and because, in accordance with the well-known tradition, Satan was unable to touch him at his birth, his *qarina* like that of

Mohammed was a good one. "On the authority of Ka'ab the Holy Spirit, Gabriel, strengthened Jesus because he was his *qarin* and his constant companion, and went with him wherever he went until the day when he was taken up to heaven."[4]

Now while in the case of Mohammed and Jesus and perhaps also in the case of other prophets, the *qarin* or *qarina* was or became a good spirit, the general teaching is that all human beings, non-Muslims as well as Muslims, have their familiar spirit, who is in every case jealous, malignant, and the cause of physical and moral ill, save in as far as his influence is warded off by magic or religion. It is just here that the belief exercises a dominating place in popular Islam. It is against this spirit of jealousy, this other self, that children wear beads, amulets, talismans. It is this other self that through jealousy, hatred, and envy prevents love between husband and wife, produces sterility and barrenness, kills the unborn child, and in the case of children as well as of adults is the cause of untold misery.

The *qarina* is believed often to assume the shape of a cat or dog or other household animal. So common is the belief that the *qarina* dwells in the body of a cat at nighttime that neither Copts nor Muslims would dare to beat or injure a cat after dark.

Many precautions are taken to defend the unborn child against its mate, or perhaps it is rather against the mate of the mother, who is jealous of the future child. Major Tremearne, who studied the subject in North Africa, says in "Ban of the Bori," the *qarin* "does not come until after the child has been actually born, for the sex is not known before that time."[5] And again:

All human beings, animals, plants, and big rocks, have a permanent soul (*quruwa*) and a familiar bori of the

same sex, and, in addition, young people have a tem-
porary bori of the opposite sex, while all living things
have two angels (*mala'ika*) in attendance. Small
stones are soulless, and so are those large ones which
are deep in the earth, "for they are evidently dead,"
else they would not have been buried. The soul has a
shape like that of the body which it inhabits, and it
dwells in the heart, but where it comes in and out of
the body is not known. It is not the shadow (*ennuwa*),
for it cannot be seen, and in fact the *ennuwa* is the
shadow both of the body and of the soul. Yet the word
quruwa is sometimes loosely used for shadow, and
there is evidently some connection, for a wizard can
pick the soul out of it. Neither is it the breath, for
when a person sleeps his soul wanders about; in fact,
it does so even when a person is day dreaming.[6]

All this, which is descriptive of the Hausa Muslims of North
Africa, closely resembles the belief in Egypt. The jinn of the opposite sex, that is, the soul mate, generally dwells underground.
It does not like its particular mortal to get married. For, again I
quote from Major Tremearne, "It sleeps with the person and
has relations during sleep as is known by the dreams." This invisible companion of the opposite sex is generally spoken of in
Egypt as "sister" or "brother." His or her abode is in quiet shady
places, especially under the threshold of the house. The death
of one or more children in the family is often attributed to their
mother's mate, and, therefore, the mother and the surviving
children wear iron anklets to ward off this danger. Most people
believe that the *qarina* dies with the individual; others that it en-
ters the grave with the body. Although the *qarina* is generally
invisible, there are those who have second sight and can see the
qarina. It wanders about at night in the shape of a cat.

The following account of the popular belief I have taken down verbatim from Sheikh Ahmed Muharram of Daghestan and recently from Smyrna. He says that his statement represents the belief of all Turkish and Russian Muslims. The *qurana* (plural of *qarina*) come into the world from the A'alam ul Barzakhiya[7] at the time the child is conceived, before it is born. Therefore during the act of coition, Muslims are told by their prophet to pronounce the word *bismillah*. This will prevent the child from being overcome by its devil and turned into an infidel or rascal. The *qarina* exists with the fetus in the womb. When the child is born, the ceremony of pronouncing the creed in its right ear and the call to prayer in the left is to protect the child from its mate.

Among the charms used against *qurana* are portions of the Koran written on lead images of fish or on leaden discs. The *qurana* are invisible except to people who are idiots and to the prophets. They often have second vision. The *qurana* do not die with their human mates but exist in the grave until the day of the resurrection, when they testify for or against the human being. The reason that young children die is because Um es Subyan (the child-witch) is jealous of the mother, and she then uses the *qarina* of the child to put an end to it.

"The way I overcome my *qarina*," said Ahmed Muharram, "is by prayer and fasting." It is when a man is overcome with sleep that his *qarina* gets the better of him. "When I omit a prayer through carelessness or forgetfulness it is my *qarina* and not myself. The *qarina* is not a spirit merely but has a spiritual body, and all of them differ in their bodily appearance, although invisible to us. The *qarina* does not increase in size, however, as does the child." The sheikh seemed to be in doubt in regard to the sex of the *qarina*. At first he would not admit that the sex relation was as indicated, thinking it improper for a man to have a female mate, but after discussion he said he was mistaken. He admitted also that all these popular beliefs were based upon the Koran and tradition, although superstitious practices had crept in among the masses.

A learned sheikh at Caliub, a Muslim village near Cairo, was also consulted on the subject. At first he tried to explain away the idea of popular Islam by saying the *qarina* referred only to the evil conscience or a man's evil nature, but after a few questions he became quite garrulous and gave the following particulars. The expectant mother, in fear of the *qarina*, visits the *sheikha* (learned woman) three months before the birth of the child and does whatever she indicates as a remedy. These *sheikhas* exercise great influence over the women and batten on their superstitious beliefs, often impersonating the *qarina* and frightening the ignorant.

The Muslim mother often denies the real sex of her babe for seven days after it is born in order to protect its life from the *qarina*. During these seven days she must not strike a cat or she and the child will both die. Candles are lighted on the seventh day and placed in a jug of water near the head of the child, to guard it against the *qarina*. Before the child is born, a special amulet is prepared, consisting of seven grains each of seven different kinds of cereals. These are sewn up in a bag, and when the infant is born, it is made to wear it. The mother also has certain verses of the Koran written with musk water or ink on the inside of a white dish. This is then filled with water and the ink washed off and the contents taken as a potion. The sheikh told me that the two last chapters of the Koran and also *Surat Al Mujadala* were most commonly used for this purpose. One of the most common amulets against the *qarina* or the child-witch is that called the "Seven Covenants of Solomon."[8]

Charms and amulets against the *qarina* abound. Books on the subject are printed by the thousands of copies. Here, for example, are the directions given for writing an amulet in the celebrated book called *Kitab Mujaribat,* by Sheikh Ahmed Ed Dirbi:

This [twenty-fourth] chapter gives an account of an amulet to be used against *qarina* and against miscarriage. This is the blessed amulet prepared to guard against all bodily and spiritual evils and against harm and sorcery and demons and fear and terror and jinn and the *qarina* and familiar spirits and ghosts and fever and all manner of illness and wetting the bed and against the child-witch (Um es Subyan) and whirlwinds and evils and poisonous insects and the evil eye and pestilence and plague and to guard the child against weeping while it sleeps—and the mystery of this writing is great for those children who have fits every month or every week or who cannot cease from crying or to the woman who is liable to miscarriage.

He continues:

And it is said that this amulet contains the great and powerful name of God—in short, it is useful for all evils. It must be written the first hour of the first day of the week, and reads as follows: In the name of God the Merciful, the Compassionate, there is no God but he, the Living, the Eternal, etc. In the name of God and to God and upon God, and there is no one victorious save God and no one can deliver him who flees from God, for he is the Living, the Self-subsisting, whom slumber seizes not nor sleep, etc. I place in the safe keeping of God him who carries this amulet, the God than whom there is no other, who knows the se-

101

cret and the hope. He is the Merciful, the Compassionate. I protect the bearer by the words of God Most Perfect and by his glorious names from evil that approaches and the eyes that flash and the souls of the wicked and from the evil of the father of wickedness and his descendants and from the evil of those that blow upon knots and from the evil of the envier when he envies, and I put him under the protection of God the Most Holy, King of the Angels and of the Spirits, Lord of the worlds, the Lord of the great throne, *Ihyashur Ihyabur Ihya-Adoni Sabaoth Al Shaddai;*[9] and I put the bearer under the keeping of God by the light of the face of God which does not change and by his eye which does not sleep nor slumber and his protection which can never be imagined nor escaped and his assistance which needs no help and his independence which has no equal and his eternity without end, his deity which cannot be overcome and his omnipresence which cannot be escaped, and I put him under the protection of the Lord of Gabriel and Michael and Israfil and Izrail and of Mohammed, the seal of the Prophets, and of all the prophets and apostles, and in the name of him who created the angels and established their footsteps by his majesty to hold up his throne when it was borne on the face of the waters, and by the eight names written upon the throne of God.

I also give the bearer the protection of K.H.T.S. and the seven H.W.M.'s and H.M.S.K's and by the talisman of M.S. and M.R. and R. and H.W.M. and S. and K. and N. and T.H. and Y.S.[10] and the learned Koran and by the name of God Most Hidden and his noble book and by him who is light upon lights, by his name who flashed into the night of darkness and destroyed by his blaze every rebellious devil and made those that feared trust him; and by the name by which man can walk upon water and make it as dry land; and by the name by which thou didst return to thy throne after the creation; and by the name by which thou didst raise up the heavens and spread out the earth and created paradise and the fire; the name by which thou didst part the sea for Moses and sent the flood to the people of Noah, the name written on Moses' rod and by which thou didst raise up Jesus, the name written on the leaves of the olive trees and upon the foreheads of the noble angels.

And I put the one who wears this amulet under the protection of him who existed before all and who will outlast all and who has created all, God, than whom there is no other, the Living, he is the Knowing and the Wise; and I put the bearer under the protection of the name of God by which he placed the seven heavens firmly and the earth upon its mountains and the waters so that they flowed and the fountains so that they burst forth and the rivers so that they watered the earth and the trees brought forth their fruit and the clouds gave rain and night became dark and the day dawned and the moon gave his light and the sun his splendor and the stars went in their course and the winds who carried his messages; and I put the bearer under the protection of the name by which Jesus spoke in the cradle and by which he raised the dead from the grave and by which he opened the eyes of those born blind and cured the lepers, the name by which he made the dumb to speak. And I protect him by the Merciful God and his great name and his per-

fect words, which neither riches nor the sinner can resist, from the evil which comes down from heaven or
the evil that ascends to heaven and from the evil
which is found upon the earth or which comes out of
the earth, and from the terror of the night and of the
day and from the oppression of the night and of the
day; and I protect him from all powerful influences of
evil and from the cursed devil and from envious men
and from the wicked infidel; and I protect him by the
Lord of Abraham the friend of God, and Moses the
spokesman of God, and Jesus, and Jacob and Isaac
and Ishmael and David and Solomon and Hob and
Yunas and Aaron and Seth and Abel and Enoch and
Noah and Elijah and Zechariah and John and Hud
and Elisha and Zu Kifl and Daniel and Jeremiah and
Shu'aib and Ilyas and Salih and Ezra and Saul and
the Prophet-of-the-fish and Lokman and Adam and
Eve and Alexander the Great and Mary and Asiah
[Pharaoh's wife] and Bilkis and Kharkil and Saf the
son of Berachiah and Mohammed the seal of the
prophets; and I protect him by God than whom there
is no other, who will remain after all things have per-
ished, and by his power and by his might and by his
exaltation above all creatures and above all devils
male and female, and all manner of jinn male and female, and familiar spirits of both sexes, and wizards
and witches, and deceivers male and female, and infidels male and female, and enemies male and female,
and ghoul and demons, and from the evil eye and the
envious, from the evil in things of ear and eye and
tongue and hand and foot and heart and conscience,
secret or open.

And I protect the wearer from everything that goes

out and comes in, from every breath that stirs of evil
or of movement of man or beasts, whether he be sick
or well, awake or sleeping, and from the evil of that
which dwells in the earth or in the clouds or in the
mountains or the air or the dust or the vapor or the
caves or the wells of the mines, and from the devil
himself, and from the flying demons and from those
who work sorcery and from the evil of the whirlwind
caused by the chief of the jinn, and from the evil of
those who dwell in tombs and in secret places, in
pools and in wells and from him who is with the wild
beasts or within the wombs, and from him who is an
eavesdropper of the secrets of the angels, etc., etc. [Af-
ter this the amulet closes with the words of the Muslim creed written three times, the call to prayer twice
and] "May God's blessing and peace be upon the
Prophet and upon his companions forever until the
day of judgment. Praise be to God the Lord of the
worlds."

All this seems the height of folly to the educated Muslim.
Yet it is taken from one of the best-selling books on popular
magic and medicine, printed in Cairo.

No one can read of these superstitious practices and beliefs, which are inseparable from the Koran and tradition,
without realizing that the belief in the *qarina* is a terror by
night and by day to pious Muslim mothers and their children.
For fear of these familiar spirits and demons they are all their
lifetime subject to bondage. In Egypt a mother never dares to
leave her infant child alone for fear of the *qarina*. The grow-
ing child must not stamp on the ground heavily for fear he
may hurt his *qarina*. It is dangerous to cast water on fire lest it
vex the *qarina*. On no account must the child be allowed to

go asleep while weeping. Its every whim must be satisfied for fear of its evil mate.

It is the firm belief in Egypt that when a mother has a boy her *qarin* (masculine) has also married a *qarina* (feminine), who at that time gives birth to a girl. This demon child and its mother are jealous of the human mother and her child. To pacify the *qarina* they sacrifice a chicken, which must be absolutely black and sacrificed with the proper ceremonies. It is impossible to see the *qarina* except in one way. Following a Jewish superstition, a man may see evil spirits by casting the ashes of the fetus of a black cat about his eyes, or by sprinkling these ashes around his bed he can trace their footsteps in the morning.

When we remember what a large percentage of the women of Egypt are unable to read, we can imagine the power that is exercised over them by the lords of this superstition, who sell amulets and prescribe treatment for the expectant mother and her child.

Al Ghazali himself in his great work, "The Revival of the Religious Sciences," in speaking of the virtue of patience, says, "He who is remiss in remembering the name of God even for the twinkling of an eye, has for that moment no mate but Satan. For God has said, 'And whosoever turns from the reminder (remembrance) of the Merciful One, we will chain to him the devil, who shall be his mate (*qarina*).'"

We may perhaps appropriately close this chapter with what one of the learned men relates regarding the victory of the believer over his demon and its powers. It may lead us to a new conception of that petition in the Lord's Prayer that we offer also for our Muslim brothers and sisters: "Lead us not into temptation, but deliver us from the evil one."

Verily, the devil is to you a foe, so take him as a foe. This is an order for us from him—may he be praised!—that we may take him as a foe. He was asked, "How are we to take him as a foe and to be delivered from him?" and he replied, "Know that God has created for every believer seven forts. The first fort is of gold and is the knowledge of God; around it is a fort of silver, and it is the faith in him; around it is a fort of iron and it is the trust in him; around it is a fort of stones and consists of thankfulness and being pleased with him; around it is a fort of clay and consists of ordering to do lawful things, prohibiting to do unlawful things, and acting accordingly; around it is a fort of emerald which consists of truthfulness and sincerity toward him: and around it is a fort of brilliant pearls, which consists of the discipline of the mind [soul].

"The believer is inside these forts and Iblis outside them barking like a dog, which the former does not mind, because he is well-fortified [defended] inside these forts. It is necessary for the believer never to leave off the discipline of the mind under any circumstances or to be slack with regard to it in any situation he may be in, for whoever leaves off the discipline of the mind or is slack in it, will meet with disappointment [from God], on account of his leaving off the best kind of discipline in the estimation of God, while Iblis is constantly busy in deluding him, in desiring for his company, and in approaching him to take from him all these forts, and to cause him to return to a state of disbelief. We seek refuge with God from that state!"[11]

107

CHAPTER
8

THE 'AKIKA
SACRIFICE

Among the many points of contact between Christianity and Islam (and the points of departure, from which the faithful missionary can launch out into the very heart of the gospel message), there is one that has not received the emphasis it deserves. I refer to the *'Akika* ceremony,* observed by every Muslim household throughout most Muslim lands after the birth of a child. Muslim traditions are full of references to this ceremony.

According to Muslim religious law, the expiatory sacrifice is made on the seventh day. It is commendable on that occasion to give the child its name, shave off the hair on its head, make an offering to the poor, and kill a victim. According to some authorities, if the offering of the *'Akika* had been neg-

---

* Commonly rendered "'*Aqiqa*."

lected on the seventh day by the parents, it can be done afterward by the child himself when he has become of age.

The root of the word 'akika is 'akka (he clave, split, rent). It is used especially in regard to the cutting off of an amulet when the boy becomes of age. It is also used in the expression "Akka bi sahmi" (he shot the arrow toward the sky), or of the sacrifice of 'Akika (he sacrificed for his newborn child).

It is interesting to note that the use of this word in every connection seems to have reference to expiation or redemption. According to Lane, the arrow as well as the sacrifice was called 'akika:[1]

It was the arrow of self-excuse. They used to do thus in the Time of Ignorance,[2] on the occasion of a demand for blood revenge. If the arrow returned smeared with blood, they were not content save with the retaliation of slaughter. But if it returned clean, they stroked their beards and made reconciliation on the condition of the blood-wit, the stroking of the beards being a sign of reconciliation. The arrow, however, as Ibu-ul-'Arabi says, did not return otherwise than clean.

The origin was this: a man of the tribe was slain, and the slayer was prosecuted for his blood, whereupon a company of the chief men collected themselves together to the heirs of the slain and offered the blood-wit, asking forgiveness for the blood. If the heir was a strong man, angered by injury, he refused to take the blood-wit. But if he was weak, he consulted the people of his tribe and then said to the petitioners: "We have, between us and our Creator, a sign denoting command and prohibition. We take an arrow and set it on a bow, and shoot it towards the sky. If it return to us smeared with blood, we are forbidden to take the

blood-wit, and are not content save with the retaliation of slaughter. But if it return clean, as it went up,
we are commanded to take the blood-wit." So they
made reconciliation.

The word 'akika in Muslim literature, however, no longer
refers to the ceremony of the arrow that belongs to the time of
ignorance. 'Akika in Muslim tradition signifies either the hair
of the young one recently born "that comes forth upon his
head in his mother's womb," or the hair of the sheep or goat
that is slaughtered as a sacrifice for the recently born infant
"on the occasion of the shaving of the infant's hair on the seventh day after his birth. The animal's limbs are divided and
cooked with water and salt and given as food to the poor."

The 'Akika sacrifice is referred to in nearly all the standard
collections of tradition, generally under Bab-an-Nikah. In
books of Fikh, it is mentioned under the head of "sacrifice"
and "offerings." The most detailed account of El 'Akika I have
found in the celebrated book on Fikh, by Ibn Rushd el
Kartabi. He treats this subject under such heads: 1. On whom
it is incumbent; 2. Where; 3. For whom it should be offered
and how many offerings should be made; 4. The time of the
ceremony; 5. Its manner; 6. What is done with the flesh.

Now in regard on whom it is incumbent, one of the
sects, namely the literalists, say that it is necessary in
every case, but most of them say it is only following
the custom of the prophet (sunna), and Abu Hanifa
says it is not incumbent and not sunna. But most of
them are agreed that he means by this that it is optional.

The reason for their disagreement is the apparent
contradiction of two traditions, namely, that a tradi-

tion of Samra concerning the prophet reads, "Every male child shall be redeemed by his *'akika,* which is to be sacrificed for him on his seventh day, and so evil shall be removed from him." This tradition would indicate that the sacrifice was incumbent. But there is the evident meaning of another tradition which reads as follows: "When Mohammed was asked concerning *El 'Akika* he said, 'I do not love *El 'Akuk* [ungrateful treatment], but to whomsoever a child is born let him make the ceremony for his child.'" This tradition infers that the custom is praiseworthy or allowable, and those who understand from it that it is praiseworthy say that the *'Akika* is *sunna,* and those who understand from it that it is allowed say it is neither *sunna* nor incumbent.

But those who follow the tradition of Samra say it is incumbent. In regard to the character of the sacrifice, all the scholars are agreed that everything that is permitted in this respect for the annual sacrifice is permitted in the case of the *'Akika* from the eight classes of animals, male and female. Malik, however, prefers the ewe as a sacrifice in his sect, and he disagrees whether the camel or the cow is sufficient. The rest of the authorities on *Fikh* say that the camel is better than the cow and that the goat is better than the sheep. The reason for their disagreement is again due to the discrepancy of tradition. For the traditions of Ibn Abbis say that the prophet of God performed the *'Akika* ceremony for Hassan and Hussain by a ram for each. Another saying of his is, "For a girl a ewe and for a boy two ewes, according to Abu Dawud."

In regard to the one for whom the ceremony is performed, the majority of them are agreed that the

'Akika should be performed for the male and the female in infancy only. The exception to this is El Hassan, who says no 'Akika shall be given for the girl, and some of them allow the 'Akika to be performed for adults.

As regards the time of this ceremony, the majority are agreed that it shall be on the seventh day after birth. Malik does not count in this number the day on which the child is born, if he is born in the daytime. Abd ul Malik, however, counts it in. Ibn el Kasim says if the 'Akika is performed at nighttime the hair of the sacrifice shall not be cut off. The companions of Malik disagree regarding the time of the cutting of the hair. It is said to be the usual time of the sacrifice, namely, forenoon. Others say immediately after dawn, basing their statement upon what is related by Malik in his Hadaya. And there is no doubt that those who permit the annual sacrifice at night permit this sacrifice also. It is also stated that the 'Akika is permitted on the fourteenth day or the twenty-first.

As regards the sunna of this ceremony and its character, it is like the sunna of the annual sacrifice, namely, that the victim must be free from blemishes as in that case, and I know no disagreement among the four schools in this respect whatever.

As regards the flesh of the victim and its skin and the other parts, the law is the same as in regard to the flesh of the annual sacrifice, both as regards eating, alms to the poor, and prohibition of sale. All authorities are agreed that formerly the head of the infant was smeared with blood in pre-Islamic times and that this custom was abrogated in Islam, basing it upon a tradition of Baridah: "In the Days of Ignorance when a

113

child was born to anyone of us, we sacrificed a sheep for him and smeared his head with its blood. When Islam came, we were accustomed at the time of the sacrifice to shave the infant's head and to smear it with saffron."

Hassan and Katadah, however, make exception to this statement, and they say that the head of the young child shall be wiped with a piece of cotton which has been dipped in the blood, and in the Days of Ignorance it was thought commendable to break the bones of the sacrifice and to cut them from the joints. And they disagree regarding the shaving of the head of the newborn child on the seventh and the alms equal in weight to the hair in silver. Some say that it is commendable; others say it is optional. Both of these opinions are based upon Malik, and I find the custom that it is commendable better. For it is based upon a saying of Ibn Habib, according to what is contained in El Muwatta: "That Fatima, the daughter of the prophet of God, shaved the hair of Hassan and Hussain and Zainab and Um Kulthum, and then she gave in alms the value of the weight in silver."

So far the summary of the ceremony according to orthodox tradition.

We turn for this account of the ceremony as given in Muslim books of jurisprudence to the present practice in Muslim lands. Herklots tells us that in India,

the 'Akika sacrifice takes place on the seventh day, called Ch'huttee, or on the fortieth day, called Chilla, in some cases on any other day that is convenient. It consists in a sacrifice to God, in the name of the child, of two he-goats if the newborn is a boy, and or one if a girl.

The he-goat requires to be above a year old, and perfect and without blemish. He must not be blind in one or both eyes, or lame, and is to be skinned so nicely that no flesh adhere to his skin, and his flesh so cut up that not a bone be broken.

Since it is difficult to separate the flesh for the smaller bones, they are boiled and dressed with the flesh remaining. While eating, the people are enjoined to chew and swallow the softer bones, and the meat is carefully taken off the larger ones without injuring the bone. The meat is well boiled, in order that it may be more easily separated from the bones. This is served up with *manda, chupatee,* or *rotee.*

While they are offering it, an Arabic sentence is repeated. The signification of which runs thus: "O Almighty God! I offer in the stead of my own offspring, life for life, blood for blood, head for head, bone for bone, hair for hair, and skin for skin. In the name of God do I sacrifice this he-goat." It is meritorious to distribute the food to all classes of people, save to the seven following individuals: the person on whose account the offering is made, his parents, and his paternal and maternal grandfathers and grandmothers. The bones, boiled or unboiled, skin, feet, and head are buried in the earth, and no one is allowed to eat them.

The custom he describes in such detail was taken by him verbatim from the lips of Jaggur Shurruf, a native of the Deccan, who belonged to the Sunni or orthodox sect. He goes on to tell us that the shaving of the head, which is called *moon-*

dun, takes place on the same day, or, in the case of the rich, the ceremony is performed some days later. Those who can afford it have the child's head shaved with a silver-mounted razor and use a silver cup to contain the water, both of which after the operation are given as a present to the barber. The hair is weighed, and its weight in silver is distributed among the religious mendicants. The hair itself is tied up in a piece of cloth and either buried in the earth or thrown in the water.

Another curious custom is thus described:

> Those who can afford it have the hair taken to the waterside, and there, after they have assembled musicians and the women, and offered *fateeha* in the name of Khoaja Khizur over the hair, on which they put flour, sugar, ghee, and milk, the whole is placed on a raft or *juhaz* (a ship), illuminated by lamps, the musicians singing and playing the whole time, they launch it on the water. Some people at the time of *moondun* leave *choontees* (or tufts of hair unshaved) in the name of particular saints, and take great care that nothing unclean contaminates them. A few, vowing in the name of a saint, do not perform *moondun* at all, but allow the hair to grow for one or even four or five years; and either at the expiration of the appointed season, or a little before or after, proceed to the *durgah* (or shrine) of that saint, and there have the hair shaved. Should it happen that they are in a distant country at that time and have not the means of repairing to his shrine, they perform *fateeha* in his name, and have the hair shaved at the place where they may happen to be. Such hair is termed *jumal choontee* or *jumal bal*. This ceremony is, by some men and women, performed with great faith in its efficacy.

According to Lane, the ceremony of 'Akika was not universal in Egypt in his day. It has become less common since. Where it is observed, a goat is sacrificed at the tomb of some saint in or near their village. The victim is called 'Akeekah and is offered as a ransom for the child from hell. The gift of the poor and the shaving of the head in all its detail as in Indian practice, however, still prevail among the villagers. The shaving of the head has been take over by the Copts and is practiced by them as well as by the Muslims. In the case of wealthy Copts a sum of money, equal in value to the weight of the hair of the infant in gold, is given to the poor. In Arabia the custom is common everywhere.

According to Doughty there is no question in the minds of the Arabs today as to the significance of the rite of sacrifice: "When a man child is born, the father will slay an ewe, but the female birth is welcomed in by no sacrifice."

In Morocco the ceremony is also well known. Says Budgett Meakin:

> On the morning of the name day, the father or nearest male relative slaughters the sheep, exclaiming as he cuts the throat, "In the name of the mighty God: for the naming of so-and-so, son (or daughter) of so-and-so," referring to the mother, who is asked to give the child a name. In the evening a feast is made of the sheep, the nurse receiving as her perquisite the fleece and a foreleg, with perhaps a present of cash besides, in return for her presence for seven days. The mother sits in state on a special chair brought by the nurse.

The custom prevails also in every part of China, although so much else of the Muslim ritual has there been modified or suppressed. A Koranic name, called King-ming, is given to the child within seven days of its birth, and a feast is celebrated. "The rich are expected to kill a sheep, two if the child is a male, and the poor are to be fed with the meat. In selecting the name the father has to hold the child with its face turned towards Mecca and repeat a prayer in each ear of the child. Then taking the Koran he turns over any seven pages, and from the seventh word of the seventh line of the seventh page gives the name."[3] Here as elsewhere the naming of the child and the 'Akika are closely related.

In Mecca, on the seventh day after the birth of a child, a wether is usually killed. According to Snouck Hurgronje, the people there do not connect this with the 'Akika ceremony, which may take place later. For the rest the ceremonies are observed by the calling of God's name in the right ear of the infant and giving the call to prayer in its left ear. A short Khutbah is given at the naming of the child and a present of silver. On the fortieth day the infant is dressed in beautiful clothes, generally of silk, and handed at sunset by the mother to one of the eunuch guardians of the Kaaba, who lays it down near the door of the Kaaba. For ten minutes the child remains under the protection of the shadow of the Kaaba. Then the mother performs the evening prayer and carries the infant home.

In the Punjab, according to Major W. Fitz G. Bourne, the ceremony is universal. He writes:

> On the sixth day after birth, the mother is bathed, all the women of the family assemble, and a feast takes place, called "Chhati." On the seventh day both male and female relations are invited, and a great feast takes place. The child's head is shaved and the hair weighed against silver, which is given to the poor. The barber places a small brass cup before the assembly, into which all present put silver.[4] A sacrifice of one or

two he-goats in the case of a male child, and of a she-goat in the case of a female child, is made. This ceremony is called "'*Aqiqa*," and is solemnized by repeating a given prayer in Arabic.

In regard to Malaysia and especially Celebes, we have interesting information from the practice prevalent among the Bare'e-speaking Toradjas, by Dr. N. Adriani and the Rev. A. C. Kruijt. They say:

The Muslims on the south coast believe that when a child dies before its third year it has no sins, and, therefore, its soul is taken directly to Allah. After the third year, however, a sacrifice is required, for a boy two goats, for a girl one. This sacrifice is called the Mosambale or '*Akika*.

The time differs, and is chiefly dependent on the prosperity of the family. If there is, however, a death in the family or the child is ill, no effort is spared to secure the necessary sacrifice. The father himself must slay the goat. If the father has died before the '*Akika* ceremony, then a portion of the father's personal possessions must be used to purchase the '*Akika* sacrifice; for example, a piece of his clothing or outfit. When the sacrifice takes place the father says: "I sacrifice the '*Akika* of so-and-so, who is the child of so-and-so. . . ." The popular opinion is that when the child dies, afterwards it rides the goat that has been sacrificed for it in order to welcome its father in the other world.

On the presentation of this sacrifice, they assert, that the future character of the child is dependent for good or for ill. The child whose morals are corrupt is

119

described as one for whom no proper '*akika* offering has been made.

In Afghanistan the practice is well known. In addition to that of the '*Akika* we learn of other vicarious sacrifices that are prevalent. Dr. Pennel says:

All Muhammadan nations must, from the origin of their religion, have many customs and observances which appear Jewish, because they were adopted by Mohammed himself from the Jews around him. But there are two, at least, met with among Afghans which are not found among neighboring Muslim people, and which strongly suggest a Jewish origin. The first, which is very common, is that of sacrificing an animal, usually a sheep or a goat, in case of illness, after which the blood of the animal is sprinkled over the doorposts of the house of the sick person, by means of which the angel of death is warded off. The other, which is much less common, and appears to be dying out, is that of taking a heifer and placing upon it the sins of the people, whereby it becomes *qurban*, or sacrifice, and then it is driven out into the wilderness.

All this testimony from many Muslim lands concerning the prevalence of a practice that is based upon the highest authority, namely *sunna*, is of course deeply interesting to the student of comparative religion. And for the theories on the subject, some of which are fanciful in the extreme, the reader is referred to such authorities as Frazer in his *Golden Bough*, or the special treatise of Professor G. A. Wilkens, "Uber das Haaropfer."

Perhaps the best explanation of the origin of this sacrifice from the standpoint of comparative religion is that given by W. Robertson Smith in his book, *Kinship and Marriage in Early Arabia.* He says:

> Shaving or polling the hair was an act of worship commonly performed when a man visited a holy place or on discharging a vow (as in the ritual of the Hebrew Nazarites). At Taif, when a man returned from a journey, his first duty was to visit the Rabba and poll his hair. The hair in these cases was an offering to the deity, and as such was sometimes mingled with a meal offering.
>
> So it must have been also with the hair of the babe, for Mohammed's daughter Fatima gave the example of bestowing in alms the weight of the hair in silver. The alms must in older times have been a payment to the sanctuary, as in the similar ceremony observed in Egypt on behalf of children recovered from sickness. The sacrifice is meant, as the prophet himself says, "to avert evil from the child by shedding blood on his behalf."
>
> This is more exactly brought out in the old usage, discontinued in Muslim time, of daubing the child's head with blood, which is the same thing with the sprinkling of the "living blood" of a victim on the tents of an army going out to battle, or the sprinkling of the blood on the doorposts at the Hebrew Passover.
>
> The blood which ensures protection by the god is, as in ritual of blood-brotherhood, blood that unites protector and protected, and in this, as in all other ancient Arabian sacrifices, was doubtless applied also to the sacred stone that represented the deity. The prophet offered a sheep indifferently for the birth of a

boy or girl, but in earlier time the sacrifice seems to have been only for boys.

For when there was no ‘acica offered the child was named and its gums rubbed with well-chewed dates on the morning after birth. The Arabs were accustomed to hide a new-born child under a cauldron till the morning light. Apparently it was not thought safe till it had been put under the protection of the deity.

I presume that in general the sacrifice, the naming and the symbolical application of the most important article of food to the child's mouth, all fell together and marked his reception into partnership in the sacra and means-of-life of his father's group. At Medina Mohammed was often called in to give the name and rub the child's gums, probably because in heathenism this was done by the priest. Such a ceremony as this would greatly facilitate the change of the child's kin. It was only necessary to dedicate it to the father's instead of the mother's god. But indeed the name ‘acica, which is applied both to the hair cut off and to the victim, seems to imply a renunciation of the original mother-kinship; for the verb ‘acca, "to sever," is not the one that would naturally be used either of shaving hair or cutting the throat of a victim, while it is the verb that is use of dissolving the bond of kindred, either with or without the addition of al-rahim.

If this is the meaning of the ceremony, it is noteworthy that it was not performed on girls, and of this the words of the traditions hardly admit a doubt.[5] The exclusion of women from inheritance would be easily understood if we could think that at one time daughters were not made of their father's kin. That certainly has been the case in some parts of the world.

In his later work, *The Religion of the Semites*, however, Professor Smith says that a fuller consideration of the whole subject of the hair offering convinces him that the name *'akika* is not connected with the idea of change of kin but is derived from the cutting away of the first hair.

> I apprehend that among the Arabs . . . the *'acica* was originally a ceremony of initiation into manhood, and that the transference of the ceremony to infancy was a later innovation, for among the Arabs, as among the Syrians, young lads let their hair grow long, and the sign of immaturity was the retention of the side locks, which adult warriors did not wear. The cutting of the side locks was, therefore, a formal mark of admission into manhood, and in the time of Herodotus it must also have been a formal initiation into the worship of Orotal,[6] for otherwise the religious significance which the Greek historian attaches to the shorn forehead of the Arabs is unintelligible.
>
> At that time, therefore, we must conclude that a hair-offering, precisely equivalent to the *'acica*, took place upon entry into manhood, and thereafter the front hair was habitually worn short as a permanent memorial of this dedicatory sacrifice. It is by no means clear that even in later times the initiatory ceremony was invariably performed in infancy, for the name *'acica*, which in Arabic denotes the first hair as well as the religious ceremony of cutting it off, is sometimes applied to the ruddy locks of a lad approaching manhood, and figuratively to the plumage of a swift young ostrich or the tufts of an ass's hair, neither of which has much resemblance to the scanty down on the head of a newborn babe. It would seem, therefore, that the

oldest Semitic usage both in Arabia and in Syria, was to sacrifice the hair of childhood upon admission to the religious and social status of manhood.

It does not seem very clear, however, that either of these theories is altogether satisfactory. Is it not more probable that we have in this Muslim custom another Jewish element in Islam connected with the Old Testament doctrine of sacrifice, especially the redemption of the firstborn (compare Exod. 13:11ff.; 22:29-30; 34:19ff.)? If, in addition to all the resemblances to the Jewish practice already noted, further testimony were necessary, it would be sufficient to refer to the statement made in the commentary on El Buchari as the key to this true Sunna of the prophet: "For the female child one ewe (and this abrogates the saying of those who disapprove a sacrifice for a girl) as did the Jews, who only made 'akika for boys."[7]

An additional proof would be the injunction of 'Ayesha, "That not a bone of this sacrifice should be broken." Surely the observation of the 'Akika ceremony may well lead us to use Exodus 12 and John 19 with our Muslim brethren, pointing them to the "Lamb of God which taketh away the sin of the world," and who is the true Redeemer also of childhood; who himself took little children into his arms and blessed them. I have recently prepared a leaflet on this subject for Muslims, entitled Hakikat ul 'Akika (The True Explanation of the 'Akika), calling attention to some of these traditions and pointing out the teaching of the Old Testament regarding the redemption by the sacrificial lamb, and showing that without the shedding of blood there is no remission of sin.

That Muslims themselves once recognized the vicarious character of this sacrifice and its deeper significance of atonement is perfectly evident from the prayer used on this occasion. In one of the books of devotion published in Hindustani and printed at Calcutta, this prayer reads as follows:

O God! This is the 'Akika sacrifice of my son so-and-so; its blood for his blood, its flesh for his flesh, its bone for his bone, its skin for his skin, its hair for his hair. O God! Make it a redemption for my son from the Fire, for truly I have turned my face to him who created the heavens and the earth, a true believer. And I am not of those who associate partners with God. Truly my prayer and my offering, my life and my death is to God, the Lord of the worlds, who has no partner, and thus I am commanded, and I belong to the Muslims.

After using this prayer the manual of devotion states that the sacrifice shall be slain by the father of the child while he cries *"Allahu akbar."*

We may well imagine that under the Old Testament law a similar intercessory prayer was offered by the pious Israelite when presenting his sacrifice on behalf of the firstborn. According to Jewish Talmudic law, every Israelite was obliged to redeem his firstborn son thirty days after the latter's birth. At the redemption the father of the child pronounces these words, "Blessed art thou in the name of him who commands us concerning the redemption of the son."

In the case of the firstborn, Jews also observe the custom of *Ahlakah,* that is, cutting the boy's hair for the first time. This took place after his fourth birthday. According to the *Jewish Encyclopedia,* it was also customary in Talmudic times to weigh the hair of the child and to present the weight in coin to the poor. According to Rabbi Joseph Jacobs, among the Beni Israel there is a custom that if a child is born as the result of a vow its hair is not cut until the sixth or seventh year. It is usual in all these cases to weigh the hair cut off and give its weight in coin to charitable purposes.

Who can fail to see that the Muslim custom is borrowed from Judaism, however much there may be mingled in the latter of early Semitic practice, the origin of which is obscure? Is there perhaps some connection also with the 'Akedah prayer and ceremony observed among the Jews?[8] The term refers to the binding of Isaac as a sacrifice, and this biblical incident plays an important part in the Jewish liturgy. The earliest illusion occurs in the Mishnah, and the following prayer is found in the New Year's Day ritual:

> Remember in our favor, O Lord our God, the oath which thou hast sworn to our father Abraham on Mount Moriah; consider the binding of his son Isaac upon the altar when he suppressed his love in order to do thy will with a whole heart! Thus may thy love suppress thy wrath against us, and through thy great goodness may the heat of thine anger be turned away from thy people, thy city and thy heritage! . . . Remember today in mercy in favor of his seed the binding of Isaac. (*Jewish Encyclopedia*)

Dr. Max Landsberg says, "In the course of time ever greater importance was attributed to the 'Akedah. The haggadistic literature is full of allusions to it; the claim to forgiveness on its account was inserted in the daily morning prayer; and a piece called 'Akedah was added to the liturgy of each of the penitential days among the German Jews." In any case we notice that among the Jews as among Muslims attempts are made to explain away the significance of this prayer and sacrifice as relating to the idea of the atonement. Accordingly, many American reform rituals have abolished the 'Akedah prayers.

It is the fashion today of liberal theology, Muslim and Jewish as well as Christian, to explain away the idea of expiation and atonement in the Old Testament as well as in the New. The altar with its blood sacrifice is as great a stumbling block to such thinkers as the cross of Christ. But the place of the altar and of the cross is central, pivotal, and dominant in the soteriology of the Bible. We cannot escape the clear teaching of God's Word, that "without the shedding of blood there is no remission of sin" (Heb. 9:22); that " the Lamb [of God was] slain before the foundation of the world" (Rev. 13:8); that the Son of God came "to give his life a ransom for many" (Matt. 20:28; Mark 10:45).

The missionary, therefore, as well as the reverent student of the Old Testament, is not satisfied with any explanation of the doctrine of sacrifice that leaves out substitution and atonement. One thing seems clear from our investigation, that we have in the 'Akika sacrifice as well as in the great annual feast of Islam with its day of sacrifice at Mecca, a clear testimony to the doctrine of a vicarious atonement and the remission of sin through the shedding of blood. Were St. Paul present at an 'Akika ceremony or at 'Arafah on the great day of the feast, would he not preach to the assembled multitudes on the remission of sins through his blood (Eph. 1:7; Col. 1:14; Rom. 5:11; 3:25)?

Surely there is pathos as well as teaching in the fact that the great Muslim world of childhood from its infancy has been consecrated to the religion of Islam by the 'Akika sacrifice.

9

ANIMISM IN THE CREED AND KORAN

O ne has only to read popular expositions on the Koran texts that refer to angels, jinn, Iblis (the devil), kismet (fate), or the many traditions regarding the creation of the soul and its transmigration to realize that the world of Muslim thought and that of animism are not distinct. Not only in popular Islam with its magic (high and low), its amulets, charms, talismans, magic squares, sacred trees, but also in the sacred literature of Islam we find pagan beliefs and practice perpetuated.

The Creed

The shortest of all monotheistic creeds, the Kalima, has it-self become a species of magic, and at least in three of the six articles of the expanded statement of orthodox belief, we find animistic teaching and interpretation: "I believe in Allah and his angels, and his books, and his prophets, and the resurrection and the predestination of good and evil." The doctrine of God includes the magical use of his names and attributes. The doctrine of angels includes not only demonology but also belief in jinn—fear and jinn worship, as real as in paganism.

The belief in revelation had in popular Islam almost degenerated into bibliomancy and bibliolatry. Do the fellahim of Egypt not take their oath on Al Bokhari? The apostles, especially Solomon and Mohammed, had communication with demons and jinn, according to the Koran and tradition. Man is created with a double ego or two souls (*qarina*), just as in the pagan mythologies. The beliefs regarding the relation of the soul to the body after death and the doctrine of metapsychosis resemble those of animism. Their belief in how the spirit leaves the body; the benefit of speedy burial; the questioning by the two angels of the tomb; the visiting of the graves and the presentation of offerings of food and drink on the graves: all this is mixed up with pagan practices that find their parallel in animism.

The Koran

We limit our discussion for the present to the use of the Koran, the creed, and the rosary in ways that are condemned by the creed itself. "There is no God but Allah"—yet his book, his names, his very attributes are used as amulets against demon and jinn or as fetish receive the worship due to himself alone. The Koran, or even portions of it, has the power of a fetish in popular Islam. Not only is the book eternal in its origin and is therefore used for mystic purposes, but only those who are pure ritually may touch it.

Certain chapters, words, or letters (e.g., *alif, lam meen*) are of special value against evil spirits. It is related in Islamic tradition that "whosoever reads the 105th chapter and the 94th chapter of the Koran at morning prayers will never suffer pain in his teeth!" This is one reason why these two chapters are almost universally used for the early prayers. At funerals they always read the chapter "Y. S.," and then for fear of jinn and spirits, the chapter of the jinn. One has only to read this last chapter with the commentaries on it to see how large a place this doctrine occupies in popular Islam. The cure for headache is said to be the thirteenth verse of the chapter called "Al-Ana' am" or the "Cattle," which reads, "His is whatsoever dwells in the night or in the day: He both hears and knows." Against robbers at night a verse of the chapter called "Repentance" is read.

No religion has ever made so much of its sacred book in a magic way as Islam. Not only do we find bibliolatry, i.e., the worship of the book, but also bibliomancy, that is the use of the Koran for magical or superstitious purposes. Much of this perhaps comes from Judaism, for the Jews also used the Torah for purposes of protection and in magical ways.[1]

The Koran is not only the most excellent of all books, but also the essential words of God contained therein are eternal and uncreated. The book was originally written by God himself on the "Preserved Tablet," then brought down in sheets to the lowest heaven on the night of Al Qadr, where they were preserved in a place called the House of Majesty (Beit-ul-'Izza). From here they were brought to Mohammed.

The Koran, once a world-reforming power, now serves to be chanted by teachers and laymen according to definite rules. The rules are not difficult, but not a thought is even given to the meaning of the words. The Koran is chanted simply because its recital is believed to be a meritorious work. This disregard of the sense of the words rises to such a pitch that even pundits who have studied the commentaries fail to notice when the verses they recite condemn as sinful things that both they and the listeners do every day, even during the very ceremony itself.

In all Muslim lands and on occasions of birth, death, and marriage, the Koran is commonly used as a charm. It is put near the head of the dying, or on the head of a newborn infant, for good luck. So holy a book can be used, therefore, even to drive away demons. No evil spirit visits the room where it rests on the highest shelf—the place of honor.

This belief in the Koran to drive away devils is exactly paralleled by practices in China. De Groot writes:

> I have said that classical works are among the best weapons in the war against ghosts. Even the simple presence of a copy, or a fragment, or a leaf of a classic is a mighty preservative, and excellent medicine for spirit-caused disease. As early as the Han dynasty, instances are mentioned of men having protected themselves against danger and misfortune by reciting classical phrases. But also writings and sayings of any kind, provided they be of an orthodox stamp, destroy ghosts and their influences. Literary men, when alone in the dark, insure their safety by reciting their classics; should babies be restless because of the presence of ghosts, classical passages do excellent service as lullabies.[2]

Again he speaks of the magical power of the Almanack:

> No house in China may be without a copy of the Almanack, or without at least its title-page in miniature, printed on purpose with one or two leaves affixed, as a

charm in accordance with the pars pro toto principle, and sold in shops for one coin or cash. These charms are deposited in beds, in corners and cupboards, and such-like places, and worn on the body and no bride passing from her paternal home into that of her bride-groom may omit the title page among the exorcising objects with which her pocket is for that occasion filled.[3]

The Rosary

In the use of the rosary (*subha*) and its gradual spread throughout the world of Islam, we also find animistic super-stition.

According to Dr. Goldziher, who has written a special es-say on the subject:

It is generally admitted that the use of the rosary, which was imported into Islam, was not adopted by the disciples of Mohammed until the third century of the Hegira. The following story can, at any rate, be cited in this connection. When the 'Abbaside Khalif Al-Hadi forbade his mother Cheizuran who tried to exercise her influence in political affairs, to take part in the affairs of state, he used the following words: "It is not a woman's business to meddle with the affairs of state; you should occupy your time with your prayers and your *subha*."

From this it seems certain that in that century the use of the *subha* as an instrument of devotion was common only among the lower classes and had no place among the learned. When a rosary was found in the possession of a certain pious saint, Abu-l-Kasim al

Junaid, who died in 297 of the Hegira, they tackled him for using it, although he belonged to the best society. "I cannot give up," said he, "a thing that serves to bring me nearer to God." This tradition furnishes us with rare facts since it shows us on the one hand that in the social sphere the use of the rosary was common even among the higher classes, and on the other hand, that the strict disciples of Mohammed looked with displeasure on this foreign innovation which was patronized by saints and pious men. To them it was 'bid' a' that is an innovation, without foundation in the old Islamic Sunna, and was consequently bound to stir a distrust among the orthodox.

Later on, when the use of the rosary had ceased to provoke discontent in the orthodox Muslims, the controversialists, whose principle was to attack all "innovations," still distrusted exaggerations in its usage. But like a great many things that were not tolerated at the beginning under religious forms, the rosary introduced itself from private religious life to the very heart of the mosques and the theological schools.

Abu Abdullah Mohammed Al-'Abdari, who died 737 A. H., wrote a work in three volumes called *Al-Madkhal*, which contains a great deal of interesting material on the intimate life of Islamic society, their superstitions, and their popular customs, and should be studied by all who are interested in the history and civilization of the Muslim Orient. "Among the innovations," writes Al-Abdari, the "rosary is to be noted. A special box is made where it is kept; a salary is fixed for some one to guard and keep it, for those who use it for Zikr. A special Sheikh is appointed for this, with the title of *Sheikh-al-Subha* and with him a servant with the title of *Khadim-al-Subha*. These innovations are quite modern. It is the duty of the imam of the mosque to suppress such customs as much as it is in his power to do so."

"The appearance of the rosary," says Goldziher (to quote again from his paper),

> and the way in which it had been adopted by the faithful did not pass unperceived by the Hadith. I believe that the following story which we read in the book called "*Sunan*" written in the third century, has to do with the entrance of the rosary:
>
> "Al-Hakam b. al-Mubarak relates on authority of Amr b. Jahja, who heard it was from his father and who in his turn had heard from his father: we were sitting before the door of 'Abdallah b. Mas'ud, before the morning prayer, for we were in the habit of going to the mosque in his company. One day we encountered Abu Musa as-Ash'ari . . . , and very soon Abu 'Abd al-Rahman came in his turn. Then Abu Musa said: 'In former times, O Abu Rahman, I saw in the mosque things that I did not approve of; but now, thank God, I see nothing but good.' 'What do you mean by that?' said the other. 'If you live long enough,' answered Abu Musa, 'you will know.' I have seen in the mosque people who sat round in circles awaiting the moment of Salat. Each group was presided over by a man and they held in their hands small stones. The President said to them, 'Repeat 100 *Takbirs*,'[4] and for a hundred times they recited the formula of the *Takbir*. Then he used to tell them 'Repeat a hundred *Tahlil*,'[5] and they recited the formula of *Tahlil* for a hundred times. Then he told them also: 'Repeat a hundred times the *Tasbih*,'[6] and the persons who were in the group equally went through this exhortation also. Then Abu

135

Abd al-Rahman asked, 'What dids't thou say when thou sawest these things?' 'Nothing,' answered Abu Musa, 'because I first wanted to find out your view and your orders.' 'Did you not tell them that it would have been more profitable for them to have kept account of their sins and did you not tell them that their good actions would not have been in vain?' So we together repaired to the mosque, and we soon came across one of these groups. He stopped before them and said, 'What do you here?' 'We have here,' they answered, 'small stones which help us to count the *Tikbir*, the *Tahlil*, and the *Tasbih*, which we recite.' But he answered them in these terms: 'Sooner count your sins and nothing will be lost of your good works. Woe to thee, O community of Mohammed! With what haste you are going toward damnation! Here are also in great numbers, companions of your Prophet. Look at these garments which are not covered with dust, these vessels that are not yet broken; verily by him who holds my soul in his hands, your religion can lead you better than the contemporaries of Mohammed; will you not at least open the door of wrong?' 'By Allah, O Abu 'Abd al-Rahman,' they cried, 'we mean but to do right!' And he answered them: 'There are many who pretend to do right, but who cannot get at it, it is to them that the word of the prophet applies: "There are of those who read the Koran, but deny its teaching, and I swear it by God, I doubt whether the majority of these people are not among yourselves."''

Other traditions show us the prophet protesting regarding some faithful women against the use of these small stones when reciting the litanies just mentioned and recommending the use of the fingers when counting their prayers.

> Let them count their prayers on their fingers (*ja'kidna bil anamil*) for an account will be taken of them.

All these insinuations found in traditions invented for the purpose, denotes a disapprobation of the use of the rosary, at the moment of its appearance. The use of small stones in the litanies was it seems an original form of the *subha*, very much like the later use of the rosary. It is said of Abu Huraira, that he cited the *Tasbih* in his house by the aid of small stones which he kept in a purse (*jusabbih biha*). Let us also mention the severe words of Abdallah, son of the khalif Omar, which he addressed to a person who rattled his stones in his hands during prayers (*juharrikk al-hasa bijedihi*): "Do not do that, for that is prompted by the devil."

Others besides Goldziher believe that the Muslim litanies were counted in this way before the rosary was introduced. One cannot be sure. In any case it seems very probable that the traditions against this custom date from the time when the rosary was introduced into Islam. The Tibetan Buddhists, long before the Christian era, used strings of beads, generally 108 in number and made of jewels, sandalwood, mussel shells, and the like, according to the status of their owners. Whether Islam adopted the rosary from India during the Muslim conquest is uncertain but not at all improbable.

Regarding the Christian use of the rosary we read:

> The custom of repeatedly reciting "Our Father" arose in the monastic life of Egypt at an early time, being

recorded by Palladius and Sozomen. The Hail Mary, or Ave Maria, on the other hand, first became a regular prayer in the second half of the eleventh century, though it was not until about the thirteenth that it was generally adopted. The addition of the words of Elizabeth, "Blessed is the fruit of thy womb, Jesus" (Luke 1:42), the angelical salutation, "Hail, Mary, full of grace; the Lord is with thee; blessed art thou amongst women" (Luke 1:28) is first mentioned about 1130. Bishop Odo of Paris (1196–1208) required the recitation of "Hail Mary" together with "Our Father" and the Creed as a regular Christian custom.

The closing petition of the rosary, "Holy Mary, Mother of God, pray for us sinners, now and at the hour of our death," developed gradually in the sixteenth century, and was regarded even by the council of Besancon (1571) as a superfluous but pious custom. These facts show that the traditions which ascribe the invention of the rosary to Benedict of Nursia, Bede, or Peter the Hermit, are untrustworthy, and the same statement holds of the Dominican tradition which speaks of a vision of the Virgin commanding the use of the rosary. At the same time, the rosary was originally an essentially Dominican mode of devotion, though first arising long after the death of the founder of the order. But while some influence may have been exercised by the acquaintance of Oriental Christians with the Mohammedan *Tasbih*, all the characteristics of the recitation of "Our Father," like the meditations connected with it, can only be explained by the operation of specifically Christian ideals.[7]

The rosary in Islam is at present used for three distinct purposes. It is used in prayer and Zikr for counting pious ejaculations or petitions. It is used for divining the will of God; and it is used in a magical way for healing.

The second practice is called *istikharah*. It is related of one of the wives of Mohammed that she said, "The prophet taught us *istikharah*, that is to know what is best, just as he taught us verses from the Book, and if any of you want anything, let him perform ablution and pray two *rakk'as* and read the verse: 'There is no other God.'" To use the rosary in this way the following things must be observed: the rosary must first be grasped within the palms of both hands, which are then rubbed together; then the *Fatiha* is solemnly repeated after which the user breathes (*nafatha*) upon the rosary with his breath in order to put the magic power of the chapter into the beads. Then he seizes a particular bead and counts toward the "pointer" bead using the words God, Mohammed, and Abu Jahal. When the count terminates with the name of God, it means that his request is favorably received, if it terminates with Abu Jahal, it is bad, and if with Mohammed the reply is doubtful. Others consider it more correct to use the three words: Adam, Eve, the devil. When these words are used, the Adam bead signifies approval, the devil bead disapproval, and the Eve bead uncertainty, because woman's judgment they say is fickle. This use of the rosary is almost universal among the common people of North Africa and Egypt.

In this connection a ceremony practiced among the Muslims of India on special occasions is worthy of mention. It is called *subha*, and usually performed on the night following a burial. The soul is then supposed to remain in the body, after which it departs to hades, there to await its final doom. The ceremony is thus described:

At night, derwishes sometimes as many as fifty assemble, and one brings a rosary of 1000 beads, each as large as a pigeon's egg. They begin with the sixty-seventh chapter of the Koran, then say three times, "God is one," then recite the last chapter but one and the first, and then say three times, "O God, favor the most excellent and most happy of thy creatures, our lord Mohammed, and his family and companions, and preserve them." To this they add: "All who commemorate thee are the mindful, and those who omit commemorating thee are the negligent."

They next repeat three thousand times, "There is no God but God," one holding the rosary and counting each repetition. After each thousand, they sometimes rest and take coffee; then one hundred times, "[I extol] the perfection of God with his praise," then the same number of times: "I beg forgiveness of God the Great," after which fifty times: "The perfection of the Lord the Eternal"; then "The perfection of the Lord the Lord of might"; etc. (Koran 37, last three verses). Two or three recite, then two or three more verses; this done, one asks his companions, "Have ye transferred [the merit of] what ye have recited to the soul of the deceased?" They reply, "We have"; and add "Peace be on the Apostles." This concludes the ceremony, which, in the house of the rich, is repeated the second and third nights.

In Algeria, the rosary is used by the Taleb in divining whether the sick will die or not. The beads are counted off in threes; if this leaves an odd number, the beads must be recounted in two, if ending evenly, the patient will live, if an odd number remains, it means death. The rosary, which is a holy thing, is never used in low magic.

In Tunisia, the fortuneteller marks a place on the rosary with a thread and counts off the beads while chanting certain words, sometimes the names of the father or mother of the sick person. The required information is founded by the number of beads remaining over after the recitation. If three remain to the thread, it is sickness. If two, it is health.

Mr. G. B. A. Gerdener, of Capetown, writes, "The rosary is sometimes worn round the neck as a cure for sickness. The kind most in use is made of sandalwood, said to come from Mecca. For magical purposes, the rosary is used by counting the beads to a certain number."

Miss G. Y. Holliday of Tabriz, Persia, gives the following information:

> The rosary is used to decide what medicine should be given, what physician should be called, whether his advice should be followed or not, etc. It is also used about all the affairs of life. It is called taking the *istikhara*. In using it, the rosary is grasped by the first bead the hand happens on; from which they count to the *Khalifa*, or the large bead which is the most prominent object, saying "bad—good," the last bead giving the decision.

In Java, the rosary is used as follows for healing the sick or for inducing sickness. With the rosary in the hand, one reads any chapter from the Koran and up to the fifteenth verse. This verse always contains a word of talismanic power, and while this verse is being read, the rosary is counted and the result follows according to the desire of the operator.

In Egypt the rosary is widely used not for divining sickness but for the cure of sickness as well. In this case, it depends on the material from which the beads are manufactured. Those

made of ordinary wood or of mother-of-pearl are not valuable,
but a rosary made of jet (*yusr*) or kuk (a particular kind of
wood from Mecca) is invaluable. In Egypt, both among Copts
and Muslims, the rosary is specially used for the cure of "re-
tention of urine" in children. It is put on the infant's neck or
is laid on the roof in the starlight to catch the dew, then it is
washed and the water given to the child to drink.

"In India," writes Mr. K. J. Khan of Poona, "the rosary is
used to protect against the evil eye, and other dangers; sometimes it is washed in water and the water given as medicine to
the sick to drink."

When we consider how in all these many superstitions,
the original use of the rosary with its ninety-nine beads for the
remembrance of the one true God has been lost or obscured,
we are forcibly reminded of the words of Warneck:

> Animistic heathenism is not a transition stage to a
> higher religion. I think I have adduced sufficient facts
> to establish that, and facts do not vanish before hypoth-
> esis. Let them produce facts to prove that animistic hea-
> thenism somewhere and somehow evolved upwards
> towards a purer knowledge of God, real facts, not imag-
> inary construction of such an evolution. Any form of
> animism known to me has no lines leading to perfec-
> tion, but only incontestable marks of degeneration.[8]

CONCLUSION

A CALL
TO PRAYER

The present condition of the Muslim world calls for prayer. We are convinced that the present apparent inability of the Christian church to deal effectively with the great problem of the evangelization of Muslims is due above all else to the weakness of the prayer life alike in the home churches and in the branches of the church that are springing up in foreign lands.

We must not forget that the supreme ministry is the ministry of prayer. It is possible for all everywhere and at all times; it is an omnipotent ministry. God is "able to do exceeding abundantly above all that we ask or think" (Eph. 3:20). "He that spared not his own Son, but delivered him up for us all, how shall he not with him also freely give us all things?" (Rom. 8:2). Prayer has proved mighty through God to the pulling down of nearly every opposing stronghold and barrier; shall it prove impotent to burst the barriers of the proudest soul and set free the captives of sin and darkness?

In the struggle for supremacy between Islam and Christianity, the statistics are all on the side of the Muslim, but the dynamics are with the Christian. To those who believe the promises of God, who know the living Christ, and have caught the vision of worldwide redemption, there can be no discouragement. We have on our side all the undiscovered wealth of God and his omnipotence.

It is our deepest conviction that the great moral and spiritual needs of the Muslim world, and the advance of Islam among pagan races, constitute an appeal to the Christian church to pray with an urgency that cannot be exaggerated, asking most earnestly that the spirit of grace and supplication in an immensely increased measure may be granted to her.

The Sword or the Cross

"The cross cannot be defeated," said Louis Massignon when he spoke to me concerning conditions in the Near East. "The cross cannot be defeated, because it itself was defeat." Long have I pondered on this mystical utterance, which sums up the history of missions in a sentence and sets forth the deepest distinction between Islam and Christianity historically considered. The cross was apparently vanquished by the sword of Islam in its wide and rapid spread throughout the Near East. Hundreds of churches became mosques, thousands of Christians apostates to Islam. Literature and architecture bowed to the genius of Mohammed and his successors. The crescent displaced the cross. But was it defeated, or does faith triumph over hope deferred?

Christ is a conqueror whose victories have always been won through loss and humiliation and suffering. He invites his followers to take up their cross as he took up his, and follow him first to their Calvary, and then to their crown. The way of the cross is the path of wisdom and of life. When we, for the sake of our Lord, suffer the loss of all things, we gain all of Christ. There can be no victory without the cross. Christ's battle flag, like that of Sigurd the Norseman, while it ensures victory to those who follow it, often brings death to those who carry it. The cross of Christ is the primal, the supreme, the central, the universal, the eternal symbol of Christianity. Christ's messengers are messengers of the cross and all it signifies, or they are not his messengers at all. "We preach Christ crucified" (1 Cor. 1:23). That is the good news that Paul says he delivered "first of all" (1 Cor. 15:3). It was his message, and it was his passion—"I am crucified with Christ" (Gal. 2:20), "I die daily" (1 Cor. 15:31).

R. W. Stewart, one of the martyr missionaries of Fukien, China, said, "The measure of your *agonia* will be the measure of your success." Xavier, before setting forth on his great mission, caught a vision of all the suffering, ignominy, and persecution before him but exclaimed, "Yet more, O Lord, yet more."

In the impending, inevitable spiritual conflict with Islam, we may perhaps expect less outward persecution of the convert to Christianity, but there will always be insidious opposition and sore secret trial for those who desert the camp of so subtle a foe. Western politics and statesmanship have never shown such timidity, such superdread of offending any religion as in the case of Islam. This too is an ominous sign on the future horizon. Therefore we must not put our trust in politics. They are uncertain at best, and whatever may prove the final adjustment of the present tangled situation, neither our hopes nor our dread lie in that direction. Our hope is in the cross. Our dread is that we should seek to escape it.

The Crusaders denied the cross by taking up the sword. "It is at this point," said Kirby Page, "that the sword and the cross differ. The sword, even used defensively, means the attempt to kill the guilty for the sake of the innocent. The cross symbolizes the willingness of the innocent to die for the guilty." The sword can only produce brutality, the cross tenderness. The sword destroys human life; the cross gives it priceless value. The sword deadens conscience; the cross awakens it. The sword ends in hatred, the cross in love. He who takes up the sword perishes by it. He who takes up the cross inherits eternal life. In winning Muslim lands for Christ, the call is for men and women who will today follow the way of the cross with the same courage and abandon with which soldiers served their countries.

The sword or the cross: self-assertion or self-denial; might or meekness; carnal weapons and methods of self-crucifixion. The friends of God, the real friends of humanity, do not hesitate in their choice. Out of weakness they are made strong; baffled they still prevail. Because they share the humiliation of the cross they too cannot be defeated. They too, as John Cordelier puts it, "are for Christ's sake wounded in the hands that work for him, in the feet that journey to him, in the heart that asks only strength to love him; as he too is wounded in his ceaseless working for us, his tireless coming to us, his ineffable desire towards us. We share the marks of his passion and he ours."

The print of the nails and the mark of the spear are still the supreme evidence of Christ's resurrection power and deity. Nay, more, these marks in ourselves are the test of our discipleship. The call is for men and women who will now offer for this sacrificial service. The old coat of arms of Tiflis, the great Muslim center in the Caucasus, is a staff of wood held by two hands. The cross is on the upper end, while below is the half moon. One hand holds the cross upright, and the other is endeavoring to uplift the half moon. Is this not typi-

146

cal of the present situation? Shall we not share the struggle by intercession?

Is Reconciliation Possible?

In spite of many discouragements, many of us are forced to the conviction that we are facing a new era, a new day, in our relations to Muslims. We believe that the hour has come when with sacrificial love and tactful sympathy we should boldly advance to win them to the allegiance of Jesus Christ.

But if we are to win our Muslim brethren for Christ, by what method are we to proceed? Our call and commission is clear and unmistakable. Archbishop Leighton said, "If our religion is false we ought to change it; if it is true we ought to propagate it." This is the implication on many a page of the gospel. It is the obligation of Christian love to share the life that we have received.

The Muslim also has his convictions and his great passion. Islam has always been aggressive. We admire the Muslim for the boldness of his faith. But have we been equally bold? God is for us. Jesus Christ has been crucified and is risen. The Spirit of Pentecost has come. All things are now ready. What wait we for? Is there any lack in God, in Christ, in the Spirit, or is the fault in us?

If we are to win our Muslim friends, what plan are we to follow? Two methods stand out in clear contrast: the polemic and the irenic; the method of argument, debate, contrast, and comparison on the one hand, and on the other hand the method of loving approach along lines of least resistance.

But some go so far as to tell us that we are to omit from our message everything that offends the Muslim mind, to avoid all criticism of Islam, and to leave out those Christian doctrines

147

and teachings that might give offense. Muslims themselves are divided on this issue. Some publicly state that Islam and Christianity can easily be reconciled; others are conscious of the deep chasm that yawns between the two systems.

Helali Bey, of Alexandria, a retired Egyptian official, who made some name as a writer and poet, published a chart some years ago, setting forth the new, conciliatory spirit of Islam. Helali Bey advocated complete union of Islam and Christianity. His ingenious chart showed the picture of a sheikh and a clergyman with hands clasped as twin brothers. He said, "The object of religion is to bring union and concord between different groups of people, to make them one whole and indivisible society; in fact, religion is behavior." He fails to see, however, that behavior depends on belief, that conduct is determined by creed.

Let us hear the other side. In a Muslim paper, *Review of Religions* (Qadian, India), the leading article was on "Christianity versus Islam," and it sounded a different note. The author, an educated Indian Muslim, stated that the ideals of Christianity and those of Islam seem outwardly the same. But beneath the surface they are very different, and there exists no possible agreement. For the Muslim idea of Deity is real and reasonable, while the Christian Deity is an inscrutable paragon of the human mind, an absurdity, a deadweight, restraining mental activity.

"The Christian plan of salvation," he says,

> is derogatory to the perfect wisdom and power of God; no sensible man can honestly accept it. . . . The Christian plan of salvation is through faith in Jesus. Mankind have fallen from their original blessedness through the sin of their first parents. They could only be saved through the vicarious office of a redeemer.

To make them fit for such a consummation God has chosen from among the nations of the earth a small tribe and made them the medium of the gradual unfolding of His scheme of salvation. While the rest of the human race remained neglected and uncared for, the chosen people were given the Law as the first installment of Divine favor and as symbol of the great mercy which was to follow. This appeared in the advent of the sinless Redeemer, "the only begotten Son of God," who to satisfy the requirements of Divine justice, offered up his own sinless life in vicarious atonement for the sins of men. A belief in him therefore entitles the believer to the benefit of the atonement.

After this frank statement of the core of Christian teaching, he goes on:

This Islamic plan, on the other hand, is rational and natural. Man is born in innocence in Islam, which is "the nature made by Allah in which he has made man" (Koran). He falls through the influence of his surroundings and by outraging his own nature. He can attain salvation only by right knowledge and right actions. There is no special favor. There is no "chosen people." God has sent teachers or prophets to all nations, who have taught their respective peoples truths regarding the purpose of human life and the way of attaining same, or in other words, truths concerning the attributes and ways of God and human conduct. Salvation is to be achieved by individual effort. "No one will bear the burden of another." There is nothing occult about the business. When by repeated good actions man realizes the goodness which is his goal, he has already achieved his salvation.

This is the Muslim gospel. It is the antipodes of our gospel.

In the ranks of Islam therefore as well as among Christians there are two views regarding the relations that are possible. Reconciliation at any price or clear reiteration of our message and investigation of the truth, cost what it may. A clash of ideas, a collision of thought, has been the inevitable result whenever and wherever Islam came into touch with Christianity.

The first conversion from Islam to Christ took place even before Mohammed died (632 A.H.). One of Mohammed's own companions left Arabia and went to Abyssinia, and there the impact of a living Christianity, although superstitious, opened the eyes of that Arab, Obeidallah bin Jahsh, so that he wrote to Mohammed, as the Arabs themselves relate, "I now see clearly, and you are still blinking." It was the same bold message that the blind man in the Gospel story gave the doubting Pharisees.

There is no reconciliation except through the atonement. That is fundamental. When we ourselves understand the mystery of the cross, and our Muslim brethren understand it, then the love of God is shed abroad in our hearts and theirs through the Holy Spirit. Without the doctrine of the cross, love degenerates into mere sentiment. With it we hear the call to sacrificial life and agonizing prayer.

How to Bridge the Chasm

Bishop Brent, writing on the work carried on among the Moros in the Philippine Islands, said, "This age-long problem of Islam has been as baffling to governments as to religion; it has a certain attractiveness just because it is so stubborn and so mysterious. Neither the Christian faith nor Christian civilization has more than dented the solid unity of Islam." The problem of Islam is perplexing and colossal. It stretches over thirteen centuries and includes many elements, all of which offer scope for study and prayer to those who are engaged in the task of interpreting Christ to Muslims.

It is a historical problem, and no one can have real sympathy with Muslims or qualify as a worker among them who has not studied the genesis of this great world movement, its wide spread, its deep penetration into language, literature, art, and architecture throughout Asia and Africa. Whether this religion has been a barrier and a stumbling block or a stepping stone and a helpful influence in the progress of the race cannot be answered offhand or categorically. The elements of the question are too many and varied.

Islam is also a political problem. When Muslim leaders sit down at conference tables with representatives of Western nations to discuss democracy, the incongruity of all this with the old idea of Islam as a church-state and with the whole Muslim theory of political government is self-evident. In spite of what has been said to the contrary, missionaries in the past realized the baffling character of the problem that Western colonial governments faced in Muslim lands. The chasm between democratic and Muslim political systems is enormous.

In its social aspects the Muslim problem involves the conditions of childhood and womanhood, the nature of life in the home, the ignorance of the masses, incredible superstitions, illiteracy, and the crying needs of the handicapped, delinquents, and dependents in Muslim society. The dark places of the Muslim world are still the habitation of cruelty. The cry of Muslim childhood is still unheeded.

The religious problem of Islam is back of it all and is therefore fundamental. The yawning chasm between the devout Muslim and the devout Christian is a problem that faces every missionary, every teacher and preacher. It is real and deep. The chasm cannot be bridged by rickety planks of compromise.

Syncretism would be equivalent to surrender. For Islam thrives only by its denial of the authority of the Scriptures, the deity of our Lord, the blessedness of the Holy Trinity, the cruciality and significance of the cross (nay, its very historicity), and the preeminence of Jesus Christ as King and Savior. And this great denial is accompanied by the assertion of the authority of another book, the Koran, the eclipse of Christ's glory by another prophet, even Mohammed, and the substitution of another path to forgiveness and holiness for the way of the cross. These denials and assertions are imbedded in the Koran and are the orthodox belief of all who know anything of their religion.

At all of these points the missionary problem is how to bridge the chasm with courage and tact, by the manifestation of the truth in love. The distribution of the Word of God always holds the first place. It has always proved its power. Not less must we flood the world of Islam with a Christian literature that is apologetic without being dogmatic, and captivating rather than polemic. We must show that the sinless human character of Jesus as recorded in the gospel forbids his classification with men. His life was in God; his principles are superhuman. He is more than an apostle.

Islam is a spiritual problem and can be solved only in spiritual terms. To the Muslim mind the unknown quantity is the exceeding greatness of the love of God in Jesus Christ, his Son, our Savior. This is the heart of the problem. Prayer and pains will accomplish wonders in solving it. In every mission station and in every missionary's prayer life this should be our chief petition: That Muslim hearts may be enlightened so that the glory of the invisible God whom they worship may be revealed to them in the face of Jesus Christ, in whom dwelleth all the fullness of the Godhead bodily. Then we shall bridge the chasm, because he will bridge it for us.

A Prayer for the Muslim World

Almighty God, our heavenly Father, who hast made of one blood all nations and hast promised that many shall come from the East and sit down with Abraham in thy kingdom: We pray for thy prodigal children in Muslim lands who are still afar off, that they may be brought nigh by the blood of Christ. Look upon them in pity, because they are ignorant of thy truth.

Take away pride of intellect and blindness of heart, and reveal to them the surpassing beauty and power of thy Son Jesus Christ. Convince them of their sin in rejecting the atonement of the only Savior. Give moral courage to those who love thee, that they may boldly confess thy name.

Hasten the day of religious freedom in Turkey, Arabia, Iran, Iraq, Afghanistan, and North Africa. Send forth reapers where the harvest is ripe, and faithful plowmen to break furrows in lands still neglected. May the tribes of Africa and Malaysia not fall a prey to Islam but be won for Christ. Bless the ministry of healing in every hospital, and the ministry of love at every church and mission. May all Muslim children in mission schools be led to Christ and accept him as their personal Savior.

Strengthen converts, restore backsliders, and give all those who labor among Muslims the tenderness of

Christ, so that bruised reeds may become pillars of his church, and smoking flaxwicks burning and shining lights. Make bare thine arm, O God, and show thy power. All our expectation is from thee.

Father, the hour has come; glorify thy Son in the Muslim world, and fulfill through him the prayer of Abraham thy friend, "O, that Ishmael might live before thee." For Jesus' sake. Amen.

NOTES

Chapter 1: The Muslim Christ

1. A. M. Fairbairn, *The Place of Christ in Modern Theology* (London, 1894), passim.
2. Cf. the refutation, in most bitter terms, of the doctrine of the Trinity in Carletti's translation of *Idhar-ul-Hak*, 1:388–417.
3. See Burhan ud Din al Halibi, *Insan al Ayoon*, and the evidence collected by Koelle, *Mohammed and Mohammedanism*, 246–52.
4. Carletti's *Idhar-ul-Hak*, "Refutation de la Trinité par les paroles de Jesus Christ," 1:396–417.
5. Mahmood bin Seyyid 'Ali, "El Khalasat el Burhanieh fi Sahet Dianet el Islamieh" (Cairo, 1319), contains it in full, with comments.
6. J. Gordon Logan, leaflet, *Islam Defies Your King!* Egypt General Mission.
7. Ameer Ali, *The Spirit of Islam*, 121–22.
8. *Mishkat*, bk. 1, chap. 3.
9. *Qarmani*, 1:70.
10. *Mishkat*, bk. 23, chap. 12.
11. Al-Damiri, *Hayat Al-Hayawan*, 227.
12. *Masnavi-i-Manavi of Jalal-ud-Din*, Whinfield's translation, 116.
13. Hughes, *Dictionary of Islam*, 235.
14. See the following chapter.
15. *Mishkat*, 2:814, Captain Mathew's translation.
16. For other passages of Scripture used by Muslims to establish that Jesus and his apostles foretold the coming of Mohammed, see Carletti's translation of *Idhar-ul-Hak*, 2:190–250.

Chapter 2: Mohammed and Christ

1. W. H. T. Gairdner, *The Reproach of Islam*, 141.
2. Titles of two chapters in the Koran.
3. On Mohammed as the foreteller of future events, see Carletti, *Idhar-ul-Hak*, 2:145–54.
4. The famous animal on which Mohammed made his night journey to heaven.
5. Quoted in W. A. Rice, *Crusaders of the Twentieth Century*, 15.
6. Cf. Samuel M. Zwemer, *Islam: A Challenge to Faith*, 48–49.
7. René Basset, *La Bordah du Cheikh el Bousiri, Poeme en l'honneur de Mohammed traduit et commentéé* (Paris, 1894), xi.
8. Cf. Carletti, *Idhar-ul-Hak*, 2:154–90; he gives forty miracles. Also, Maulvi Mohammed Inayat Ahmad, *Two Hundred and Fifty-two Authentic Miracles of Mohammed*, translated and published by the Mohammedan Tract and Book Depot (Lahore, 1894).
9. Cf. recent Muslim literature in Egypt, especially Ahmed Ali El Malyee's *Jawab'an Su'al badh Ahl-el-kitab*.
10. The Shiah sect also believe that Mohammed has superseded Jesus Christ and is superior to him in station and dignity, but they add that Ali also is in every respect not only the equal of Jesus Christ but superior to him. See, for example, the book entitled *Munakib al Abtal*, by Mohammed bin Ali bin Shar Ashub (Bombay).
11. *Edinburgh Conference Report*, 4:147.

Chapter 4: Christianity's Stumbling Block

1. Goldziher, *Mohammedanische Studien*, vol. 2.
2. Cf. Samuel M. Zwemer, *The Moslem Christ*, 78–112.
3. Hans Visscher, *Across the Sahara*, 168.
4. W. A. Rice, *Crusaders of the Twentieth Century*, 252.
5. Koelle, *Mohammed and Mohammedanism*, 3:310, 334.
6. *Mishkat* 18.3.
7. Sir Lewis Pelly, *The Miracle Play of Hassan and Hussein*, 2:343–48.
8. James Denny, *The Death of Christ*, 302.

Chapter 5: The Way to the Muslim Heart

1. Anders Nygren, *Agape and Eros: A Study of the Christian Idea of Love*, 3 vols. (London: S.P.C.K., 1938).

2. Whinfield's translation, 116.

3. Compare the Koran text on the subject.

Chapter 6: Animism's Influence

1. Rabbi Geiger, "Was hat Mohammed aus dem Judenthume aufgenommen" (Wiesbaden, 1833).

2. Rev. K. W. S. Kennedy, *Animism* (Westminster, 1914).

3. Warneck, *The Living Christ and Dying Heathenism*, 7.

4. Cf. Charles E. G. Tisdall, *The Sources of the Qur'an*, 44–45.

5. Snouck Hurgronje, *The Achenese*, trans. A. W. S. O'Sullivan (Luzac and Company, 1906), 287–88.

6. Gottfried Simon, *The Progress and Arrest of Islam in Sumatra* (London, 1912), 157–59.

7. Ibid., 48–51.

8. Skeat, *Malay Magic*, xiii.

9. Warneck, *Living Christ and Dying Heathenism*, 103.

10. *Encyclopedia Britannica*, "Animism."

11. Charles E. G. Tisdall, *The Missionary Review of the World*, 1916.

12. Simon, *The Progress and Arrest of Islam in Sumatra*.

13. Harnack, *The Mission and Expansion of Christianity*, vol. 1, bk. 2, chap. 3.

Chapter 7: The Familiar Spirit or *Qarina*

1. Palmer's translation is used throughout.

2. "Book of the Dead," 1:73.

3. Ibn-Khallikan, quoted in *Hayat Al-Hayawan*, "Jinn."

4. Eth Tha'alabi, "Kasus el Anbiya."

5. Major Tremearne, "Ban of the Bori," 97.

6. Ibid., 131.

7. The unseen world, hades, the abode of souls after death and before birth.

8. A translation of this appears in Samuel M. Zwemer, *The Disintegration of Islam* (New York: Fleming H. Revell and Company, 1916).

9. This portion shows Jewish origin and gives some of the Hebrew names of God.

10. These are mystical letters that occur in the Koran text.

11. Al Damiri, *Hayat Al-Hayawan*, 1:470 (English translation by Jayakar).

Chapter 8: The 'Akika Sacrifice

1. Lane, *Arabic-English Lexicon*, vol. 5., sub voce.
2. The expression "the Time of Ignorance" refers to the period before the introduction of Islam.
3. Marshall Broomhall, *Islam in China*.
4. This is also the custom in Egypt.
5. On the contrary, the traditions leave the matter uncertain except as regards the practice of the Jews.
6. *Orotal—Allah Ta'ala*, God Supreme.
7. 'Araki in Tirmidhi, *Fath-ul-Bari*, 5:390.
8. *'Akedah*—the binding or knotting of a rope.

Chapter 9: Animism in the Creed and Koran

1. See *Jewish Encyclopedia*, 3:202–3.
2. DeGroot, *The Religion of the Chinese*, 51.
3. Ibid., 53.
4. *Takbir*—to repeat *Allahu Akbur*, "God is great."
5. *Tahlil*—to repeat *Lailaha illa Allah*, the creed.
6. *Tasbih*—to repeat *Subhan Allah*, "God be praised."
7. *Schaff-Herzog Encyclopedia*, vol. 10.
8. Warneck, *The Living Christ and Dying Heathenism*, 10.

INDEX OF SCRIPTURE

INDEX OF SUBJECTS
AND NAMES

161

165